Deprivation and Social Comparison

Dr. Asoke Kumar Saha
B.Sc. (Hons.), M.Sc. (Thesis), Rajshahi University
D.Phil., University of Allahabad, India
Professor
Department of Psychology
Jagannath University, Dhaka

Prints Publications Pvt Ltd
New Delhi

Published by

Prints Publications Pvt Ltd
Viraj Tower-2, 4259/3, Ansari Road,
Darya Ganj, New Delhi-110002
Tel. : +91-11-45355555
Fax: +91-11-23275542
E-mail : contact@printspublications.com
Website : www.printspublications.com

First Edition : 2022 (Hardbound)

ISBN 978-81-927694-7-9

Price : ₹ 495/-

Published and Printed by Mr. Pranav Gupta (Director) on behalf of Prints Publications Pvt Ltd at Mohit Enterprises, Delhi.

ABOUT THE BOOK

This book is an outcome of a major review on deprivation and social comparison started from 1950s and onward. This present book has described the introduction of deprivation, different theories of relative deprivation, relative deprivation and social movement, Bowlby's psychological understanding of deprivation, Augustine's views of deprivation, social deprivation, relative and absolute deprivation, theoretical construct of relative deprivation, definition of relative deprivation theory, cultural deprivation, political deprivation, economic deprivation, critical analysis of deprivation studies, and deprivation of liberty and its critical understanding in relation to social, economic and political deprivation. The book also discussed the consequences of deprivation and social comparison along with examples and reality in different culture and geographical locations.

The book also focuses on the relative deprivation of Hindus among different caste systems (Brahmin and Sudra) in Bangladesh. The results provided confirmation to all hypotheses formulated. It was found that regardless of sex and residential background, Brahmin participants expressed higher gratification and Sudra participants expressed higher deprivation. A two-way interaction involving caste and sex was statistically significant. A three-way interaction involving caste, sex and residential background was also statistically significant. Brahmin male participants expressed significantly higher gratification as compared to female participants. Whereas Sudra male participants perceived significantly higher fraternal relative deprivation as compared to female participants.

Dedicated to

The Memory of My Father Late Dr. Santosh Kumar Saha,

My Mother Late Mira Rani Saha

and

All My Family Members

Contents

Page No.

Preface (*vii*)

Executive Summary 1–4

1. Introduction and Theoretical Understanding of Deprivation 5–52

1. Introduction
2. What is relative deprivation
3. Relative deprivation and social movement
4. Bowlby's psychological understanding of deprivation
5. Augustine's views of deprivation
6. Social deprivation
7. Relative and absolute deprivation
8. Theoretical construct of relative deprivation
9. Definition of relative deprivation theory
10. Cultural deprivation
11. Political deprivation
12. Economic deprivation
13. Critical analysis of deprivation studies
14. Deprivation of liberty

2. Socio-Cultural Background of Bangladesh and West Bengal 53–63

1. West Bengal and Bangladesh
2. Partition of India
3. Partition of and Emergence of Bangladesh

3. Emergence and Development of Hindu Caste System 64–66

1. Rationale of the study
2. Hypothesis

4. Development and Objectives of the Study 67–73

1. Analysis and Results

5. Methods and Practices 74–77

1. Design
2. Sample
3. Mode of sample selection
4. Material Used
5. Procedure

6. Analysis and Results 78–80

1. Main effects
2. Interaction effect

7. Discussion and Conclusion 81–85

Bibliography 87–99

Preface

I am humbly expressing my indebtedness to late Professor Dr. Mozammel Huq, Department of Psychology under whom the study was carried out by me. I also express my deep sense of gratitude to Professor Huq, the then Chairman, Department of Psychology, for guiding my research work and giving me constructive suggestions. In fact, this was the first research study I conducted so far at my post-graduate level. I have no hesitation in admitting that I could not have finished my work in time without his active participation and timely guidance in various phases of the research work.

Let me extend my heartfelt honor to my Doctoral Research Supervisor an eminent Professor E.S.K. Ghosh, Department of Psychology, Allahabad University, India who works closely with Henry Tajfel at Bristol University, UK. He is also a mentor of my life and found him as a man of excellence and wisdom. I am also grateful to Professor Dr. R.C. Tripathi and Professor Dr. Janak Pandey, Department of Psychology, Allahabad University for their constant support, encouragement and advice in academic activities.

Let me congratulate Professor Dr. Mijanur Rahman, the Honorable Vice Chancellor of Jagannath University, and Professor Dr. Kamaluddin Ahmed, Treasurer of Jagannath University for their constant support in academic and administrative activities. I also want to extend my gratitude to Professor Dr. Kazi Saifuddin who is an academic leader and publish the highest number of psychological books in Bangladesh. I am also grateful to my colleague Professor Dr. Noor Muhammad, Chairman, Department of Psychology, Jagannath University with whom I share lots of academic issues and I found him a readymade reference in psychology.

I am especially thankful to my uncle Mr. Arbainda Kar, Retd. Secretary, Ministry of Power and Mineral Resources, Government of Bangladesh who always encouraged me for my academic accomplishment. I also want to extend my profound thanks to my late father Dr. Santosh Kumar Saha and my mother late Mira Rani Saha who is my constant source of inspiration. Very special thanks are due to my wife Smt. Ujjala Saha and my beloved son Artho Saha for allowing me sacrificing their valuable time to complete the manuscript of this book.

ASOKE KUMAR SAHA
The Author

Executive Summary

This book is an outcome of a major research investigation conducted at the Department of Psychology, Rajshahi University. This book has describe the introduction of deprivation, what is relative deprivation, relative deprivation and social movement, Bowlby's psychological understanding of deprivation, Augustine's views of deprivation, social deprivation, relative and absolute deprivation, theoretical construct of relative deprivation, definition of relative deprivation theory, cultural deprivation, political deprivation, economic deprivation, critical analysis of deprivation studies, and deprivation of liberty and its critical understanding in relation to social, economic and political deprivation.

The present study was designed to investigate empirically the phenomenon of fraternal relative deprivation in Brahmin with high caste identity and Sudra with low caste identity as related to male-female categorization and urban-rural origin. The study was based on several theoretical construct of relative deprivation as conceived by Runciman (1966), Gurr (1970), Davis (1959) and Martin (1981). The term relative deprivation may be egoistic or fraternal. When the deprivation occurs on individual level, it is called egoistic relative deprivation. When the deprivation happens on group level, it is called fraternal relative deprivation.

The broad objective of the study was to explore the phenomenon of fraternal relative deprivation as related to caste, sex and residential background of Hindus in Bangladesh. Specific objectives of the study were as follows:

1. To show differential pattern of fraternal relative deprivation in Brahmins and Sudras due to social, political, and economic discrimination.
2. To show the patterns of deprivation in Brahmins and Sudras due to male-female categorization.
3. To compare between various forms of relative deprivation in Brahmins and Sudras as a result of urban-rural residential background.
4. To study fraternal relative deprivation in Brahmins and Sudras in relation to social, economic and political conditions of Bangladesh.

The sample of the study constituted 200 participants equally divided into Brahmins and Sudras. Each group of Brahmins and Sudras was equally divided into males and females. Each group of males and females was again subdivided into rural and urban origin. All the participants were students between 20 to 25 years old. They were collected from Rajshahi University, Rajshahi Government College, and Rajshahi Medical College. All the participants were students of graduate levels.

Fraternal relative deprivation scale was used as instruments for the collection of data. The scale contained 9 items of which 3 items were in political area, 3 items were in economic area and 3 items were in social areas. The hypotheses formulated for the study were as follows:-

1. Brahmins participants with high caste identity would feel gratification and Sudra participants with low caste identity would feel deprivation in their

competitions for social, economic and political privileges.

2. (*a*) In case of Brahmins, males would express higher feelings of gratification in comparison to females; (*b*) In case of Sudra, females would express higher feelings of fraternal relative deprivation in comparison to males.
3. Residential background in terms of urban and rural origin would have differential impact on gratification as well as deprivation of the participants.

The results provided confirmation to all hypotheses. It was found that regardless of sex and residential background, Brahmin participants expressed higher gratification and Sudra participants expressed higher deprivation. A two-way interaction involving caste and sex was statistically significant. A three-way interaction involving caste, sex and residential background was also statistically significant. For Brahmin, male participants expressed significantly higher gratification as compared to female participants. For Sudra, male participants perceived significantly higher fraternal relative deprivation as compared to female participants.

Furthermore, urban male participants of Brahmin origin perceived highest gratification followed by rural male, urban female and rural female participants. In contrast, rural male participants of Surda origin perceived highest fraternal relative deprivation followed by urban female, urban male and rural female participants. A comparison on each dimension showed that Brahmin urban male participants expressed significantly higher gratification as compared to rural female participants in economic areas. But Brahmin rural male participants expressed significantly higher gratification as compared to their female counterparts in social areas. However, no significant mean differences were obtained by Brahmin participants on gratification scores and by Sudra participants on deprivation scores in political areas.

In conclusion, it can be said that the study was not amply sufficient to explore the multi-facet aspects of relative deprivation. To understand the phenomenon of fraternal relative deprivation in Bangladeshi Hindus, it is necessary to utilize multi-dimensional factors and it needs extensive empirical verification.

CHAPTER 1

Introduction and Theoretical Understanding of Deprivation

Introduction

Deprivation might be defined as losing something in which a person once had, whereas privation might be defined as never having something in the first place. Deprivation is the state of being deprived of that which is needed for "normal life".

In psychology it might refer to- maternal deprivation, Cultural deprivation, Environmental deprivation, Food deprivation maternal deprivation, Poverty, REM dream deprivation and Sensory deprivation.

What is Relative Deprivation?

Let's say that it's Christmas and your parents just bought you a brand new iPhone. You've wanted this phone for a long time, and you were so excited to receive it as a gift. A few days after you get the phone you decide to go to your friend's house to show it off a little bit. When you get there, you find out that your friend's parents bought him a brand new car. How do you feel about your phone now? Are you still as happy as you were before? If you feel a little jealous of your friend or are not as happy with your gift, you are experiencing relative deprivation. Relative deprivation is the belief that a person will feel deprived or entitled to something based on the comparison to someone else. In this case, the point of reference would be your friend who now possesses a new car. Since you don't have a car, this becomes a new desire and something you wish to acquire.

Relative deprivation is the lack of resources to sustain the diet, lifestyle, activities and amenities that an individual or group are accustomed to or that are widely encouraged or approved in the society to which they belong. Measuring relative deprivation allows an objective comparison between the situation of the individual or group compared to the rest of society. Relative deprivation may also emphasize the individual experience of discontent when being deprived of something to which one believes oneself to be entitled; however emphasizing the perspective of the individual makes objective measurement problematic.

It is a term used in social sciences to describe feelings or measures of economic, political, or social deprivation that are relative rather than absolute. The term is inextricably linked to the similar terms poverty and social exclusion. The concept of relative deprivation has important consequences for both behavior and attitudes, including feelings of stress, political attitudes, and participation in collective action. It is relevant to researchers studying multiple fields in social sciences. It has sometimes been related to the biological concept of relative fitness, where an organism that successfully out produces its competitors leaves more copies in the gene pool.

Social scientists, particularly political scientists and sociologists, have cited 'relative deprivation' (especially temporal relative deprivation) as a potential cause of social movements and deviance, leading in extreme situations to political violence such as rioting, terrorism, civil wars and other instances of social deviance such as crime. For example, some scholars of social movements explain their rise by citing grievances of people who feel deprived of what they perceive as values to which they are entitled. Similarly, individuals engage in deviant behaviors when their means do not match their goals. Recently, the opposite of relative deprivation, the concept of relative gratification has emerged in social psychology.

Relative Deprivation Theory and Social Movement

Relative Deprivation theory is credited to sociologist Samuel Stouffer, who developed the approach while studying social psychology during World War II. Stouffer found that soldiers of that era measured their personal success not with the standards set by the military but on the experience they had within their individual units. Take, for example, a private in the Military Police and an Air Force private. In addition to their rank, they both also have the same level of education and have been in the military for the same amount of time. Despite their likenesses, the Air Force private feels a sense of deprivation due to the nature of rapid promotions in the Air Force; he has not acquired a promotion yet and feels deprived. However, the private in the Military Police does not have this same sense of deprivation because in his unit promotions are not as prevalent. This conclusion made a tremendous impact on the field of sociology and would later be used to explain social movements and revolutions. A social movement is a form of group action, either formal or informal, that aims to change a political or social issue. As social movement theory (or the study of social mobilization) emerged, scientists made the connection between relative deprivation and people assembling for social change.

The doctrine of relative deprivation sustained by American scholars (Gurr 1970) has led some projects on agitation and mass movements. Relative deprivation is described as player's recognition of inconsistency between their value desires and their environment's manifest value potentialities. Value prospects are the goods and conditions of life to which people suppose they are fairly entitled.

The determinants of value potentialities are to be appeared extensively in the social and physical surroundings; they are the stipulations that decide people's known possibilities of obtaining or retaining the norms they justifiably desire to achieve. Gurr comments: "The frustration - aggression and the related treat - aggression mechanisms provide the basic motivational link between Relative Deprivation and the potential for collective violence." Gurr also tie three other points to relative deprivation, namely dissonance, anomie and conflict. The second of the concepts anomie is significant in its effect to estimate opportunities. There are three exemplary in order to draw the classification of value expectations and value potentialities have influence on relative deprivation. Decremented deprivation ideal explains the situation where the desires are firm but capabilities deteriorate. In aspiration model, J –curve or progressive deprivation model, adapts to the situations when expectations and capabilities first enhance together but then capabilities cease to incase or decrease even when expectations carry on proceeding.

Those who observe deprivation and as a consequence realize an impression of disappointment become violent.

They are 'jealous' of those who possess more. They protest or revolt against those who have more. They do not take measures to resolve the problem related to the sources of deprivation. Gurr treats 'deprivation' as primarily psychological; thus he does not handle the socio-economic framework, which is the origin of deprivation. If such sense of deprivation is confined to an individual against another individual it leads to crime. When it is transformed to collective transformation a deprivation of region, community or caste– it assumes the shape of collective activity. But it is not escorted with ideology for the social system; it lies to be a remonstration or agitation and rarely takes a form of social movement. They put on 'temporary aberration' in place of 'ongoing processes of change.'

Relative deprivation is an important but not an adequate factor for protest movements. M.S.A. Rao contends, 'a sufficient level of understanding and reflection is required on the part of the participants, and the must be able to observe and perceive the contrast between the social and cultural conditions of the privileged and those of the deprived, and must realize that it is possible to do something about it.'

Bowlby's Psychological Understanding of Deprivation

In 1950s and '60s British psychiatrist John Bowlby discovered that humans have an innate motivational system independent from feeding and sexuality, and equally important for survival, which he called attachment behavioural system. Humans share with other species a drive to create and maintain an intimate, affectionate bond with a particular other identified as able to better cope with the world, and thus provide security and protection. Attachment behaviour is aimed at maintaining proximity to this close other who in infant's case is one, or very few of his or her primary caregivers, and with whom the infant seeks contact especially when in distress.

Bowlby discovered that the infant's need for love is just as important as their need for food, and correspondingly deprivation of love or sensitive, warm and continuous care is just as damaging as food deprivation. The latter leads to starvation; the former leads to the death of the soul, as psychiatrist James Gilligan eloquently put it, from outside an attachment perspective. In the language of Bowlby's theory, deprivation or frustration of attachment needs through caregivers' delayed or lack of response, unavailability, negligence, rejection, absence, or abuse is conducive to children's development of an "affectionless and delinquent character." Deprived children grow up to reiterate in their social interactions the same patterns of behaviour that they experienced and learnt in early childhood, thus perpetuating the cycle of violence, and some of them being later on diagnosed as psychopaths or classified as violent offenders.

The disruption or brutalization of affectionate bonds deprived children are overwhelmed with conflicting emotions (e.g., fear, desire, anxiety, anger) and, in the absence of a safe environment where they can express these emotions and of a sensitive caregiver who can attune to their emotional states and soothe them, they are provided with no strategy to regulate emotion and cope with stress and difficult situations. They do not feel free to express anger as a protest behaviour because they fear both the one towards whom the anger is directed (their caregiver) and the increase in distance between them and their caregiver that may result from communicated anger, and which threatens their survival. This unprocessed and unregulated anger predisposes them to over reactive and violent behaviour, and the constant sense that the world is not safe conditions them to perceive threats in their relational environment even when they are not there and consequently respond with angry, aggressive, and hostile behaviour. There is evidence that early childhood deprivation relates to criminality later in life, and severely deprived or attachment-disordered children have been noted to display traits of the adult psychopathic and antisocial personality, such that they have been described as "violent psychopaths in training." Already in 1951 Bowlby cautioned that: "Deprived children, whether in their own homes or out of them, are sources of social infection as real and serious as are carriers of diphtheria and typhoid." In contrast, secure attachment relationships with primary caregivers protect the child from developing anti-social, violent patterns of thinking, acting, and interacting.

There is currently abundant attachment research attesting to the link between early childhood deprivation (and the correspondent formation of insecure attachment patterns) and the increased risk for both perpetration and receipt of relationship violence. 12 Bowlby observed that the person in therapy may alternatively adopt one or other of the two basic forms of behaviour that they learnt in childhood, that of parents towards them and that of themselves towards parents, which means that insecurely attached or deprived individuals can shift from the role of the victimizer to that of the victim, depending on context. In fact, the two roles are just as intimately connected as the child is to his or her main caregiver and both are learnt in this primary relationship. Not surprisingly, studies revealed that there is a propensity for abusiveness in victims of relationship violence and that the victim's own violent behaviour and feelings of aggression need to be acknowledged and addressed in therapy so that they would be better managed.

Within this framework, I want to single out two important aspects of the psychological theory of deprivation: first, that in most cases the perpetrator of violence is also a victim of violence, and second, that violence springs from a lack. As shown by Duniec and Raz, Bowlby was inspired by the medical model of deficiency disease to base attachment theory on the concept of lack, thus bringing to the fore the importance of a psychological lack (emotional deprivation) which is no less grave than a physiological lack (e.g., malnutrition). 16 I therefore want to point out that a basic issue is how this lack can be understood, and depending on that, how it can be healed or treated. Attachment theory answers this from a multidisciplinary perspective, including knowledge and evidence from neurology, biology, ethnology, psychology, and psychoanalysis, which is then accommodated to various therapeutic views and methods. I propose that a philosophical concept of deprivation can be usefully integrated with this framework and serve both to the understanding and treatment of violence seen as rooted in deprivation.

Augustine's Views of Deprivation

In the late fourth and early fifth century CE, Augustine advanced an ontological theory of 'evil' as 'lack' or 'deprivation of the good,' complemented by an ethical view of evil as 'disorder' of will. To Augustine every being or individual substance possesses ontological goodness, i.e., it is good by the very fact that it is, since everything that is has the intrinsic and valuable attributes of measure, form, and order. 18 There is no substance or nature that is evil in itself although one may relate to others in ways that lack agreement (a scorpion may sting me), or one may choose to act wrongly towards others (I may harm someone through the exercise of a disordered will). Being is in itself a good (though not a moral good) to things that possess it and as possessed by them: the very fact that I exist as a human being is a good for me, irrespective of my actions being good or bad towards others. Rational beings can diminish their ontological goodness or fullness of being through morally bad choices, which acted-out allow for the existence of evil. Actions however are not substances (things that exist independently, in themselves), and thus evil exists as a relation between substances, with no being of its own. Evil is that which deprives a being of its corresponding integrity, making it be less, which is why Augustine refers to evil as 'deprivation of the good' (privatio boni) or being less (minus esse).

For Augustine evil as 'deprivation of the good' represents a lack of some-thing which ought to be there in the deprived being, a lack of a substantial quality which properly belongs to it, whether it be one previously possessed or one whose due acquisition failed. Evil is in a being falling short of realizing its proper form, or coming to be underdeveloped with respect to its nature. In attachment theory, too, the negativity of deprivation is acknowledged by pointing to something being absent, something that individuals were supposed to have but failed to have due to early developmental, relational, care giving failures. Deprived individuals are lacking in abilities related to cognition (memory, learning, language), personal agency, and emotion, as they are little apt to regulate emotions (such as fear, rage, shame, despair) and to experience emotions (such as empathy, compassion, remorse, faith, trust). From a neurological viewpoint, they lack neural connections which fail to be formed in the right hemisphere during infancy due to the miss attunement between themselves and their caregiver. The inadequate development of neural structures in the limbic and para-limbic systems and the orbit frontal cortex, which is responsible for the modulation of affect and social behaviour, impairs individuals' capacity to empathies, self-regulate, and perceive the emotional and mental states of others, and consequently predisposes them to impulsive and violent responses. These anatomical and psychological lacks are the result of a child's experiencing the inadequate, sometimes aggressive behaviour of primary caregivers, and are also the developmental origin of violent behaviour in recipients of such treatment.

Augustine's notion of being less, of diminishment in one's fullness of being speaks however of the ontological negativity of deprivation, pointing us to consider that in deprived individuals the lacks go beyond the biological and psychological levels, pervading their ontological structure: the inner constitution of what makes a human be what a human is. To Augustine, the human being is (as any other substance) a unity of parts and capacities which come together in different degrees of internal integration. The more one's capacities are formed and in orderly function, and thus in accord with each other, the more being one has; the more they lose form and order, the more one's being lessens.

A methodological note is appropriate at this stage: in order to explore how Augustine's notion of ontological deprivation can complement the psychological understanding of deprivation and be of use to therapists, the view of human beings as substances has to be accepted as one that holds therapeutic value and not necessarily one that is correct in itself. I find that a philosophy of substance can still be compelling today, but regardless of which philosophical argument prevails (for or against there being substances), I contend that it is useful for clinicians (whether psychotherapists or physicians) to accept a theoretical framework where persons are treated as substances. The reason for this is that persons in their care do have a sense that they are an ineffable coherent unity, non-reducible to their bio-neuropsychological processes, and that that unity is broken in them. If the persons they treat conceive of themselves, reflectively or non-reflectively, as substances, then there is a clear advantage for clinicians to do the same, but I want to suggest that the advantage is still there regardless of how persons in therapy think of themselves.

For one who takes Augustine's line on ontological deprivation, a person may have a fully formed brain and fully functional biological system to support their psychological processes and still have pervasive lacks in their ontological structure, defined by Augustine as esse-nosse-velle, being-knowing-willing. Our being, reason and will are basic constituents of our nature because they are immediately accessible to us, and through nothing other than themselves: because I am a living creature I perceive myself as living; I know anything, including that I have a mind and what the mind is, through the mind itself; and I move towards things and use them through the will which moves and uses itself. Thinking with Augustine, one who is not psychologically and neurologically deprived can nonetheless subject oneself to ontological deprivation, diminishing one's capacities for reason and will (through their repeated misuse), and thus decreasing in form and order, or lessening one's being. Or, one can have some of the lacking neurological connections formed through therapy (which is what attachment-focused therapy aims at), and still continue to be ontologically deprived in their intellectual and volitional capacities, and consequently subject themselves to further deprivation. The opposite situation is also possible: the fundamental ontological capacities can resist deprivation even when one is subjected to neuropsychological lacks that are considered to engender violent behaviour. This is more easily achieved in adulthood, but looking through Augustine's framework can perhaps offer an explanation for why not all children subjected to psychological deprivation grow up to be dysfunctional, violent, or deeply troubled human beings: despite possible neurological lacks, their ontological capacities underwent enough formation to allow for fairly adequate psychological functioning.

Within Augustine's discourse reason lessens and disrupts the ontological order when it goes against its nature and lets itself be ruled by senses, instead of just getting information from senses and working with it. The consequence of such disorder is that reason allows for lacks to pervade it, loses its ontological fullness, and compromises its good functioning. The same happens when the will goes against its ontological goodness and internal unity by turning towards bad choices, and generating morally failed actions. Enacted wrong choices ontologically diminish the will, because they emerge from the will's failure to realize itself according to its good nature. Inordinate will and reason generate ontological deprivation, a decrease in being, which causes further psychological (and moral) disorder, affecting the quality and cohesion of one's volitions (divided, weakened wills), emotions (misdirected passions, desires, affections), and cognitions (failed sensible and intellectual knowledge), and resulting in morally faulty actions and defective modes of operating that enhance ontological deprivation. "Inasmuch as we are, we are good' (in quantum sumus, boni sumus), writes Augustine, and "to the extent that we are bad, we are less" (in quantum mali sumus, in tantum etiam minus sumus). On ontological level, as human beings, we remain always good, even when diminished; on psychological level inordinate choice and action generate disorder, malfunctioning, and moral failure, which produce ontological diminution. From this viewpoint, when the unity and integrity of capacities which makes us be what we are (human beings) is disrupted instead of being further formed, it is not just our psychological processes of reasoning and willing that are impaired but also our substantial capacities for reason and will, correspondent to our nature.

Social Deprivation

The term "social deprivation" is slightly ambiguous and lacks a concrete definition. There are several important aspects that are consistently found within research on the subject. With social deprivation one may have limited access to the social world due to factors such as low socioeconomic status or poor education. The socially deprived may experience "a deprivation of basic capabilities due to a lack of freedom, rather than merely low income." This lack of freedoms may include reduced opportunity, political voice, or dignity (https://en.wikipedia.org/wiki/Social_deprivation).

Part of the confusion in defining social deprivation seems to stem from its apparent similarity to social exclusion. Social deprivation may be correlated with or contribute to social exclusion, which is when a member in a particular society is ostracized by other members of the society. The excluded member is denied access to the resources that allow for healthy social, economic, and political interaction. Pierson has identified five key factors that set social exclusion in motion–poverty, lack of access to jobs, denial of social supports or peer networks, exclusion from services, and negative attitude of the local neighborhood. It is also associated with abusive caretaking, developmental delay, mental illness and subsequent suicide. Although a person may be socially deprived or excluded, they will not necessarily develop mental illness or perpetuate the cycle of deprivation. Such groups and individuals may have completely normal development and retain a strong sense of community.

Relative and Absolute Deprivation

Some sociologists, for instance Karl Polanyi, have argued that relative differences in economic wealth are more important than absolute deprivation, and that it is more significant in determining human quality of life. This debate has important consequences for social policy, particularly on whether poverty can be eliminated simply by raising total wealth or whether egalitarian measures are also needed. A specific form of relative deprivation is relative poverty. A measure of relative poverty defines poverty as being below some relative poverty line, such as households who earn less than 20% of the median income (https://en.wikipedia.org/wiki/Relative_deprivation).

This refers to a theory of social change that attributes drastic events like social and political revolutions to the desire among a group of people within society to acquire the privileges that are enjoyed by other privileged groups. In other words, social change is seen as the result of the feeling of deprivation or other forms of serious discontent experienced by a group of people. Relative deprivation could be caused by economic or other social inequalities among various social groups. It is believed that group members who were earlier dispersed may find common ground in a cause that leads them to ignore their individual interests and unite under a single cause.

Critique : Critique of this theory has pointed out that this theory fails to explain why some people who feel discontent fail to take action and join social movements. Counter-arguments include that some people are prone to conflict-avoidance, short-term-oriented, and that imminent life difficulties may arise since there is no guarantee that life-improvement will result from social action.

Quotations : Consider also this quotation from Karl Marx: "A house may be large or small; as long as the neighboring houses are likewise small, it satisfies all social requirements for a residence. But let their arise next to the little house a palace, and the little house shrinks to a hut. The little house now makes it clear that its inmate has no social position at all to maintain, or but a very insignificant one; and however high it may shoot up in the course of civilization, if the neighboring palace rises in equal of even in greater measure, the occupant of the relatively little house will always find himself more uncomfortable, more dissatisfied, more cramped within his four walls."

Theoretical Construct of Relative Deprivation

Runciman (1966) has given the basic components of relative deprivation theory. He has stated that a person is relatively deprived of any valued object when four conditions are presents. For example, a person does not have 'X', he sees other persons as having 'X'. Now the person wants 'X' and he thinks that he should have 'X' because he has the necessary qualities and abilities to possess 'X'. Thus, according to Runciman relative deprivation has two dimensions such as magnitude and degree. Magnitude is the participative extent while degree is the emotional intensity with which deprivation is felt.

Gurr (1970) has defined relative deprivation as an individual's perception of a discrepancy between his value expectations and value capabilities. Value expectations were defined as those goods and conditions to which actors believe they are rightfully entitled. Value capabilities are those, which they think they are capable of getting and keeping. According to Gurr, value expectations do not necessarily depend upon the value attainments of reference to others, but can arise from a variety of specifiable sources. Finally, Gurr proposed that variation on intensity and score of relative deprivation in a collectivity would be strongly related to its potential for collective violence. On the basis of these explanations of relative deprivation theory Gurr (1970) has postulated that both level of anticipated future relative deprivation and anticipated increase in relative deprivation may predispose people to collective violence. Further, he has suggested that increase in relative deprivation from past to present will also lead to collective violence. It means that any change in relative deprivation present and future will be associated with greater political protest behavior.

Martin (1981) explained relative deprivation in terms of four variable models. These are (*a*) pattern of distribution of rewards, (*b*) the comparison process, i.e. egotistic or fraternal, (*c*) feeling of deprivation, and (*d*) resulting behavior. A formal theory of relative deprivation was introduced by Davis (1959). This theory states that if a person desires an object and perceives similar others possess that object, then he experiences a sense of injustice. This results in the feeling of deprivation. Thus, the felt relative deprivation means that a person who lacks 'X', he wants 'X', and he feels entitled to 'X'. When anyone of these dimensions is lacking, deprivation does not occur.

In Bangladesh context, Huq (1988) conducted an empirical investigation to explore the phenomenon of fraternal relative deprivation and intergroup behavior in the social context of Bangladesh. A factorial design involving three levels of dimensions of deprivation (i.e. political/social/economic), three levels of socio-economic status (i.e. high/middle/low), and two levels of ethnic groups composition (majority/minority) was utilized. A linear pattern of relationship emerged for both gratification and deprivation for the respective majority and minority groups. It seemed to suggest a closer correspondence for perceived deprivation or gratification corresponding to socio-economic status levels. In another study, Huq (1991) explored the phenomenon of fraternal relative deprivation of Bangladeshi students as related to Sex and Residential background. These findings show that the socio-economic and political context of Bangladesh has generated a lot of complexities in understanding fraternal relative deprivation. The results of this study showed that male subjects expressed significantly higher feelings of gratifications and female subjects expressed significantly higher feelings of deprivation. Furthermore male subjects of urban and rural background showed significantly highest feelings of gratifications in political areas as compared to social and economic areas. But female subjects of urban and rural background expressed significantly highest feelings of deprivation in political areas. On the basis of these findings, the investigator concluded that the feelings of social injustice and the perception of unequal social status might be responsible for giving birth to the phenomenon of fraternal relative deprivation.

Huq and Saha (1992) have investigated environmental effect on perceived fraternal relative deprivation. Results show that both physical and social environment was found to account for perceived fraternal relative deprivation of Hindus in Bangladesh in differential amounts. It seems to indicate that both physical and social environment independently can profoundly influence the nature of fraternal relative deprivation of Hindus in Bangladesh. Tripathi and Srivastava (1981) reported that in India relatively deprived Muslims had more positive ingroup attitudes as well as more negatives outgroup attitudes than those of Muslim who did not feel relative deprivation.

A critical review of these theoretical explanations of the concept of relative deprivations shows that Davis, Runciman and Gurr differ among themselves on certain points. For example, Davis did not mention about the feasibility of the object. But Runciman added that the individual must think that it is feasible to obtain the object, 'X'. In contrast to Runciman, Gurr claimed that an individual experiences deprivation only when he thinks that it is not feasible to obtain 'X'. It is thus clear that three theories of relative deprivation as proposed by Devis, Runciman and Gurr differ with respect to the elements of feasibility. For Runciman, deprivation exists when the perceived feasibility is high. For Gurr, deprivation exists when perceived feasibility is low. For Davis, feasibility is irrelevant. In a word, it may be said that Gurr has created a more dynamic model of relative deprivation than Davis or Runciman. Gurr differs from Runciman in that he has focused on the consequences of deprivation while Runciman is more interested in the antecedents.

The empirical research findings about relative deprivation and its correlates as reported here were conducted in different countries and in varied situations. These research findings show that relative deprivation in general and fraternal relative deprivation in particular may emerge due to social injustice, racial discrimination, unequal distribution of resources and discriminative treatment to one group by another group. All these aspects of relative deprivation were utilized in the present study.

One study suggests that the higher rates of crime found amongst young people from socio-economically disadvantaged families reflect a life course process in which adverse family, individual, school, and peer factors combine to increase individual susceptibility to crime. Human deprivation is lack of human capabilities, opportunities, choices, values and access to basic needs such as food, shelter, cloth, health, education etc.

Membership in a group may contribute to the development of positive or negative social identity of an individual. People generally compare their own membership group to some other reference group. This comparison is made on some evaluative dimensions which have clear value differentials (Commins and Lockwood, 1979). This comparison may result in legitimate or illegitimate perception of the group. Legitimate means favorable and illegitimate means unfavorable comparisons. This may be stable or unstable. When the individuals make unfavorable comparisons and it is judged to be both illegitimate and stable, it is said to be in a state of relative deprivation.

Thus, the concept of relative deprivation is a kind of social evaluation theory (Pettigrew, 1967). It formalizes the relationships between social comparison groups. It leads to a variety of behavioral outcomes, when the individual's evaluation proves to be negative, the individual experiences relative deprivation. Then he is motivated to change the membership or to change the dimensions of comparison or he is directed towards revolution for changing the existing social system. The initial concept of relative deprivation was introduced by Stouffer and colleagues (1949), followed by Davis (1959) and Runciman (1966). Runciman distinguishes between Egoistic Relative Deprivation (ERD) and Fraternal Relative Deprivation (FRD). When the individual compares himself with other of his own group and feels deprived in relation to them, it is called egoistic relative deprivation. Fraternal relative deprivation involves the comparison of the ingroup to an out-group and the conclusion is that the ingroup is deprived. The present study is concerned with an empirical investigation of Fraternal Relative Deprivation as related to caste, sex and residential background of Hindus in Bangladesh.

Definition of Relative Deprivation Theory

In sociology, relative deprivation theory is a view of social change and movements, according to which people take action for social change in order to acquire something (for example, opportunities, status, or wealth) that others possess and which they believe they should have, too. Some sociologists believe relative deprivation theory explains why people join social movements or advocate social change. For example, in this view, gay people join the movement for gay marriage in order to acquire something (the right to marry) they believe others already possess; relative to these people, such advocates of gay marriage believe they are deprived. Critics claim that relative deprivation theory does not explain why some people join movements that apparently do not benefit them directly (animal rights movements, say).

Deprivation is distinguishable into relative and absolute deprivation. Physical abuse, starvation, and poverty are seen as forms of absolute deprivation, whereas relative deprivation can be defined as the discrepancy between what one expects in life and what one gets. Both absolute and relative deprivations are causes of the deprived one's receptivity to particular (religious) messages: "Come to me, all you who labor and are heavy laden, and I will give you rest" (St Matthew 11:28).

Relative deprivation theory and research proposes that people use comparisons with other people, groups, or themselves at different points in time to evaluate their current circumstances. If these comparisons lead people to believe that they do not have what they deserve, they will be angry and resentful. Relative deprivation (RD) describes these subjective evaluations.

Deprivation was seen by generations of scholars, not necessarily Marxists, as the cause of both personal religious commitment and sect and cult formation. The German scholars Max Weber and Ernst Troeltsch were pioneers with regard to the relationships between sect and church membership, and social class and status group. In The Social Sources of Denominationalism (Holt 1929), H. Richard Niebuhr saw sects as the "churches of the disinherited"; because of their lack of economic and political power, the less privileged needed religion most, and sects and cults could provide their members with compensation for the lack of social and personal success.

In the 1950s and 1960s, much theorizing centered on the construction of typologies. This was also the case in deprivation theory. For example, Charles Glock (1964, Glock and Stark 1965) distinguished five types of deprivation, depending on the kinds of strain felt: economic, social, organismic, ethical, and psychic deprivation. Every type gave rise to a particular type of religious group, respectively: sect, church, healing movement, reform movement, or cult. According to the class into which it fell, Glock could predict the "career" of the particular religious group. According to Bryan Wilson (1973), most new religious movements in the Third World were both thaumaturgic- that is, they responded to very specific and acute forms of deprivation- or revolutionist- to the strain felt by the putative imminent destruction of the world.

Since the 1970s, deprivation theory has been criticized by various scholars. Its main defect is that, although the ideology component in the recruitment of members is rightly stressed, class is but one of the many factors that affect religious commitment. Another serious defect is the absence of any social network consideration. These shortcomings can be met when deprivation theory is integrated into a more full-fledged theory. This can be done, as was demonstrated by Stark and Bainbridge (1987), for example, in their formal, rational choice theory on religious behavior.

Relative deprivation is the experience of being deprived of something to which one believes oneself to be entitled. It refers to the discontent people feel when they compare their positions to others and realize that they have less of what they believe themselves to be entitled than those around them.

Schaefer defines it as "the conscious experience of a negative discrepancy between legitimate expectations and present actualities. It is a term used in social sciences to describe feelings or measures of economic, political, or social deprivation that are relative rather than absolute. In the recent days, marginalization in education refers to educational deprivation.

The concept of relative deprivation has important consequences for both behavior and attitudes, including feelings of stress, political attitudes, and participation in collective action. It is relevant to researchers studying multiple fields in social sciences. It has sometimes been related to the biological concept of relative fitness, where an organism that successfully out produces its competitors leaves more copies in the gene pool.

Social scientists, particularly political scientists and sociologists, have cited 'relative deprivation' (especially temporal relative deprivation) as a potential cause of social movements and deviance, leading in extreme situations to political violence such as rioting, terrorism, civil wars and other instances of social deviance such as crime. For example, some scholars of social movements explain their rise by citing grievances of people who feel deprived of what they perceive as values to which they are entitled. Similarly, individuals engage in deviant behaviors when their means do not match their goals.

American sociologist Robert K. Merton was among the first (if not the first) to use the concept of relative deprivation in order to understand social deviance, using French sociologist Emile Durkheim's concept of anomie as a starting point.

In one of the first formal definitions of the relative deprivation, Walter Runciman noted that there are four preconditions of relative deprivation (of object X by person A):

- Person A does not have X
- Person A knows of other persons that have X
- Person A wants to have X
- Person A believes obtaining X is realistic

Runciman distinguishes between egoistic and fraternalistic relative deprivation. The former is caused by unfavorable social position when compared to other, better off members of a specific group of which A is the member) and the latter, by unfavorable comparison to other, better off groups. Egoistic relative deprivation can be seen in the example of a worker who believes he should have been promoted faster and may lead that person to take actions intended to improve his position within the group; those actions are, however, unlikely to affect many people. Fraternalistic can be seen in the example of racial discrimination, and are much more likely to result in the creation and growth of large social movement, like the American Civil Rights Movement in the 1960s. Another example of fraternalistic relative deprivation is the envy teenagers feel towards the wealthy characters who are portrayed in movies and on television as being "middle class" or "normal" despite wearing expensive clothes, driving expensive cars, and living in mansions.

Deprivation Theory means that people who are deprived of things deemed valuable in society—whether money, justice, status or privilege—join social movements with the hope of redressing their grievances. This is a beginning point for looking at why people join social movements; however, it is even more important to look at relative deprivation theory, a belief that people join social movement based on their evaluations of what they think they should have compared with what others have. On the contrary, absolute deprivation is people's actual negative condition; relative deprivation is what people think they should have relative to what others have, or even compared with their own past or perceived future. Improved conditions fuel human desires for even better conditions, and thus can spark revolutions.

Feelings of deprivation are relative, as they come from a comparison to social norms that are not absolute and usually differ from time and place. This differentiates relative deprivation from objective deprivation (also known as absolute deprivation or absolute poverty) - a condition that applies to all underprivileged people. This leads to an important conclusion: while the objective deprivation (poverty) in the world may change over time, relative deprivation will not, as long as social inequality persists and some humans are better off than others.

Consider the following examples: in 1905 cars were a luxury, hence an individual unable to afford one would not feel or be viewed as deprived. In 2010, when cars are common in most societies, an individual unable to afford one is much more likely to feel deprived. In another example, mobile phones are common today, and many people may feel that they deserve to have one. Fifty years ago, when there were no mobile phones, such a sentiment would obviously not exist.

Relative deprivation may be temporal; that is, it can be experienced by people that experience expansion of rights or wealth, followed by stagnation or reversal of those gains. Such phenomena are also known as unfulfilled rising expectations.

In an example from the political realm, the lack of the right to vote is more likely to be felt as a deprivation by people who had it once than by the people who never had the opportunity to vote.

Relative deprivation is the experience of being deprived of something to which one believes to be entitled. It refers to the discontent people feel when they compare their positions to others and realize that they have less of what they believe themselves to be entitled than those around them.

- Some scholars of social movements explain their rise by citing grievances of people who feel deprived of what they perceive as values to which they are entitled. Similarly, individuals engage in deviant behaviors when their means do not match their goals.
- Feelings of deprivation are relative, as they come from a comparison to social norms that are not absolute and usually differ from time and place.
- Critics of this theory have pointed out that this theory fails to explain why some people who feel discontent fail to take action and join social movements.

In a study Heather J. Smith found that relative deprivation (RD) is the judgment that one is worse off compared to some standard accompanied by feelings of anger and resentment. Social scientists use RD to predict a wide range of significant outcome variables: collective action, individual achievement and deviance, intergroup attitudes, and physical and mental health. But the results are often weak and inconsistent. The authors draw on a theoretical and meta-analytic review (210 studies composing 293 independent samples, 421 tests, and 186,073 respondents) to present a model that integrates group and individual RD. RD measures that (*a*) include justice-related affect, (*b*) match the outcome level of analysis, and (*c*) use higher quality measures yield significantly stronger relationships. Future research should focus on appropriate RD measurement, angry resentment, and the inclusion of theoretically relevant situational appraisals. Such methodological improvements would revitalize RD as a useful social psychological predictor of a wide range of important individual and social processes.

Relative Deprivation first coined by Sam Stouffer and his associates in their wartime study The American Soldier (1949), relative deprivation was rigorously formulated by W G Runciman in 1966. Its use in criminology was not until the 1980s by theorists such as S Stack, John Braithwaite and particularly the left realists (see entry) for whom it is a key concept. Its attraction as an explanatory variable in the post-war period is because of the rise of crime in the majority of industrial societies despite the increase in living standards. That is, where material deprivation in an absolute sense declined and the old equation of the more poverty the more crime was clearly falsified.

Relative Deprivation occurs where individuals or groups subjectively perceive themselves as unfairly disadvantaged over others perceived as having similar attributes and deserving similar rewards (their reference groups). It is in contrast with absolute deprivation, where biological health is impaired or where relative levels of wealth are compared based on objective differences - although it is often confused with the latter. Subjective experiences of deprivation are essential and, indeed, relative deprivation is more likely when the differences between two groups' narrows so that comparisons can be easily made than where there are caste-like differences. The discontent arising from relative deprivation has been used to explain radical politics (whether of the left or the right), messianic religions, the rise of social movements, industrial disputes and the whole plethora of crime and deviance.

The usual distinction made is that religious fervor or demands for political change are a collective response to relative deprivation whereas crime is an individualistic response. But this is certainly not true of many crimes - for example, smuggling, poaching or terrorism - which have a collective nature and a communal base and does not even allow for gang delinquency which is clearly a collective response. The connection is, therefore, largely under-theorized- a reflection of the separate development of the concept within the seemingly discrete disciplines of sociology of religion, political sociology and criminology.

The use of relative deprivation in criminology is often conflated with Merton's anomie theory of crime and deviance and its development by Cloward and Ohlin, and there are discernible, although largely unexplored, parallels. Anomie theory involves a disparity between culturally induced aspirations (e.g. success in terms of the American Dream) and the opportunities to realize them. The parallel is clear: this is a subjective process wherein discontent is transmuted into crime. Furthermore, Merton in his classic 1938 article, 'Social Structure and Anomie', clearly understands the relative nature of discontent explicitly criticizing theories which link absolute deprivation to crime by pointing to poor countries with low crime rates in contrast to the wealthy United States with a comparatively high rate. But there are clear differences; in particular Mertonian anomie involves an inability to realize culturally induced notions of success. It does not involve comparisons between groups but individuals measuring themselves against a general goal. The fact that Merton, the major theorist of reference groups, did not fuse this with his theory of anomie is, as Runciman notes, very strange but probably reflects the particular American concern with 'winners' and 'losers' and the individualism of that culture. The empirical implications of this difference in emphasis are, however, significant: anomie theory would naturally predict the vast majority of crime to occur at the bottom of society amongst the 'losers' but relative deprivation theory does not necessarily have this overwhelming class focus. For discontent can be felt anywhere in the class structure where people perceive their rewards as unfair compared to those with similar attributes. Thus crime would be more widespread although it would be conceded that discontent would be greatest amongst the socially excluded.

The future integration of anomie and relative deprivation theory offers great promise in that relative deprivation offers a much more widespread notion of discontent and its emphasis on subjectivity insures against the tendency within anomie theory of merely measuring objective differences in equality (so called 'strain' theory) whereas anomie theory, on its part, offers a wider structural perspective in terms of the crucial role of differential opportunity structures and firmly locates the dynamic of deprivation within capitalist society as a whole.

Runciman's Relative Deprivation and Social Justice (Routledge, 1966) is the best exposition of the concept and his in-depth exploration of its dimensions could form a rich source for future criminological theory. What is to be Done About Law and Order? By John Lea and Jock Young (London: Pluto, 1993) has an extensive discussion of relative deprivation as a cause of crime. For a thorough examination of the literature on relative deprivation interpreted in a more objectivist way (ie by measuring income disparities and assuming there is subjective discontent) see S Box Recession, Crime and Punishment (Macmillan, 1987). Jock Young's The

Exclusive Society (Sage, 1999) traces the transformation of relative deprivation in late modernity and the likely impact of this on the quality and nature of crime.

Cultural Deprivation

Cultural Deprivation is a term referring to the absence of certain expected and acceptable cultural phenomena in the environment which results in the failure of the individual to communicate and respond in the most appropriate manner within the context of society. Language acquisition and language use are commonly used in assessing this concept.[1]

Proponents of this term argue that the culture of the people in the working class (regardless of race, gender, ethnicity and other factors) is inherently deficient and different from the middle class. According to this theory, this deprivation results in the working class remaining always poor and unable to leave their class to higher classes.

Cultural Deprivation refers to the social class structure of society. How the middle class gain cultural capital via primary socialization compared to that of the working class who have been socialized differently without this culture capital. Culture capital is what helps the middle class succeed in the capitalist system of society; the norms and values the middle class lean help their educational achievement and employability. The working class members of society that lack culture capital do not pass it on to their children, reproducing the class system (Willis (1977) Learning to Labour). Morais Suggests that middle class children's culture capital allows them to communicate with their middle class teachers more effectively than the working class children which Morias *et al.* suggest is a contributor in the inequality between social classes.

With arguments from Bourdieu (understanding Bourdieu 2004 webb *et al.*) that state schools are set up to make everybody middle class whereby only the middle class and some high achieving working class can achieve this. Continuing his argument that exams suit the middle class, academic work meets the strengths of the middle class leaving the working class trying to meet the expected standards of others strengths with their weaknesses. The culture deprivation from a Marx perspective suggests that the material and resources available to the working class is limited, thus are educated poorly before entering the first steps of education. Some pupils start school with the ability to read at a low level, some can't even write their name. This shows the difference in opportunity and values that create a culture deprivation for the working class at a very early age.

Political Deprivation

The Deprivation of Political Rights is an accessory punishment defined in the Criminal Law of the People's Republic of China (Article 34 of Chapter III), which can be enforced solely or with a principal penalty (e.g. capital punishment or life sentence) to limit the convicted person's right to be involved in political deprivation. The Deprivation of Political Rights is an accessory punishment defined in the Criminal Law of the People's Republic of China (Article 34 of Chapter III), which can be enforced solely or with a principal penalty (e.g. capital punishment or life sentence) to limit the convicted person's right to be involved in political activities. For those sentenced to a principle penalty with deprivation of political rights, the deprivation is effective during their time incarcerated and the duration as sentenced from the day of their release or parole. It is only automatically imposed on those sentenced to life imprisonment or death penalty. If the principle penalty is commuted, usually so will the deprivation of political rights. Political rights are not automatically deprived for prisoners, and those inmates who are not subject to this deprivation can and do still vote and theoretically can even be elected.

Economic Deprivation

According to the family stress model, economic deprivation induces psychological distresses such as, depression, anxiety, and parental stress, due to the strain of having fewer resources available for day-to-day living. Strong associations exist between poverty in early childhood and problem behavior in later life (e.g., Dearing *et al.*, 2006; Sun *et al.*, 2015; Mazza *et al.*, 2016). While not all children living in economic hardship go on to display conduct problems, a disproportionately high number of children with conduct problems tend to come from families living in poverty (Boe *et al.*, 2012). Evidence from longitudinal studies (e.g., Kiernan and Huerta, 2008; Rijlaarsdam *et al.*, 2013) have identified poverty in early childhood as a risk antecedent to problem behavior across the lifespan. Additionally, experimental and longitudinal findings demonstrate that changes in family income directly lead to changes in child conduct problems (Costello *et al.*, 2003; Morris and Gennetian, 2003; Votruba-Drzal, 2006). While these findings suggest a causal link between poverty and conduct problems, the mechanism by which economic deprivation leads to conduct problems remains unclear.

Two theoretical perspectives that have been extensively deployed to explain this mechanism are the family stress model and the investment model (Mayer, 1997; Conger *et al.*, 2010). Both theories posit an indirect effect of poverty on childhood conduct problems. Boss *et al.* (2017, p. 4) defined family stress as "a disturbance in the study state of the family system." Such a disturbance may be due to external factors such as, unemployment or internal factors such as, divorce. Others (e.g., McCubbin *et al.*, 1980) have conceptualized family stress as the response of a family to distressing life events and tensions generated by these events. According to the family stress model, economic deprivation induces psychological distresses such as, depression, anxiety, and parental stress, due to the strain of having fewer resources available for day-to-day living. Such stressors are associated with frustration and aggressive interactions (Berkowitz, 1989) which in turn lead parents to adopt punitive or unresponsive parenting styles with consequences for childhood conduct trajectories (Conger *et al.*, 2010). Support for this model comes from studies demonstrating a link between poverty, parental psychological distress, punitive discipline, and conduct problems (Gershoff *et al.*, 2007; Kiernan and Huerta, 2008; Rijlaarsdam *et al.*, 2013).

Family investment on the other hand is defined as the amount of money parents put into purchasing quality education, nutrition, health, good neighborhood, and other inputs that improves a child's future well-being (Mayer, 2002). This investment is determined by a family's income. The investment model proposes that poverty restricts parents' ability to provide enriching educational experiences and services, as well as sufficiently nutritious diets. This in turn leads to lower cognitive abilities with potential consequences for other developmental domains (Mayer, 1997; Conger *et al.*, 2010). Economic deprivation has been found to longitudinally predict low educational investment and consequently cognitive abilities (Kiernan and Huerta, 2008; Sun *et al.*, 2015). Additionally, changes in parental economic circumstances predict investment in nutritious diets (Skafida and Treanor, 2014), and childhood malnutrition has been linked to low cognitive ability and conduct problems in adolescence (Galler *et al.*, 2012).

Recent extensive reviews of the application of the family stress and investment models show that very few studies (e.g., Guo and Harris, 2000; Yeung *et al.*, 2002) have simultaneously integrated elements from the two models in understanding a single developmental outcome such as, conduct problems (Conger *et al.*, 2010; Shaw and Shelleby, 2014). Most studies employing both models in a single study have used them to explain different outcomes, that is, the family stress model being used to explain behavioral outcomes and the investment model to explain cognitive outcomes (e.g., Gershoff *et al.*, 2007; Kiernan and Huerta, 2008). Where both models have been used to explore pathways from poverty to conduct problems (e.g., Linver *et al.*, 2002; Rijlaarsdam *et al.*, 2013), these were not directly predicted from the main consequence of low investment, that is, cognitive ability. It is well established that poverty directly stunts the development of those cognitive competences (e.g., executive function, language, working memory, and decision making) that underpin children's emotional and self-regulatory responses (Noble *et al.*, 2005; Farah *et al.*, 2006), mechanisms that are directly linked to conduct problems or tendency to take on prosocial roles such as, standing up to bullies (Belacchi and Farina, 2010; Montroy *et al.*, 2014). Concurrent association studies have also found that cognitive ability predicts conduct problems (e.g., Bellanti and Bierman, 2000). Further, Galler *et al.* (2012) found that the effect of childhood malnutrition on conduct problems in adolescence was mediated by cognitive ability. It is therefore no surprise that interventions aimed at improving cognitive ability and underpinning processes such as, emotional regulation also lead to improvements in child conduct problems or gains in prosocial behavior, and those aimed at improving behavior result in cognitive benefits (Lunkenheimer *et al.*, 2008; Scott *et al.*, 2010; Ornaghi *et al.*, 2017). In other words, an investment pathway from poverty to conduct problems should include cognitive ability as a key mediator.

Closely linked to the above are calls to explore other pathways between poverty and childhood outcomes within the context of these models. For instance, Shaw and Shelleby (2014) argued for the testing of a direct path between parental distress and childhood conduct problems, beyond the indirect effect through parenting because associations between parental distress and conduct problems may depend on factors other than compromised parenting. One argument is that maternal psychological distress can have direct effects on childhood conduct problems through heritability of negative traits linked to conduct problems during pregnancy (Goldsmith *et al.*, 1997; Kim-Cohen *et al.*, 2005). According to Shaw and Shelleby (2014), parental stress during pregnancy can induce neuroendocrine alterations which in turn lead to development of negative traits, such as, irritability, associated with conduct problems. Other researchers have documented direct effects between economic deprivation and conduct problems (Kiernan and Huerta, 2008), suggesting that the effect of poverty may not be completely mediated by family stress and investment variables.

Further, researchers have critiqued the limited use of longitudinal data in testing these models among children (Conger *et al.*, 2010; Shaw and Shelleby, 2014). We came across only one study that used data matching the temporal ordering of predictors, mediators and outcome variables (i.e., Rijlaarsdam *et al.*, 2013). Additionally, only one recent longitudinal study using the family stress model (e.g., Mazza *et al.*, 2016) have examined the effect of deprivation on conduct problems over time, and we are not aware of any study combining both stress and investment mediators to examine conduct problems over time.

Critical Analysis of Deprivation Studies

Empirical studies relating to Fraternal Relative Deprivation are mainly concerned with intergroup conflicts. A large number of studies have identified fraternal relative deprivation as underline causes for revolution, political unrest, industrial tensions, and ethnic conflicts. For the purpose of the present study, a short review of relevant literature relating to fraternal relative deprivation is given below.

Stauffer and his colleagues (1949) introduced the concept of relative deprivation through their study of the American soldiers. They found that relative deprivation in American soldiers was due to dissatisfaction in various cadres and highest relative deprivation was evident in those cadres where promotions were restricted. Runciman (1966) made an extensive study of the British working class and found his participants to express egoistic relative deprivation. Runciman, however contends that the fraternal relative deprivation can instigate social action and it is caused by the feelings of social injustice.

Street and Legget (1961) found that the measure of fraternal relative deprivation was better predictor of riot participation by black Americans. Pettigrew (1964) has also furnished systematic evidence that fraternal relative deprivation was a much stronger predictor of black unrest in America. Pettigrew (1967) also found that greatest reluctance to support black political candidates was found among those whites who were fraternally deprived.

Searles and Williams (1962) showed that black students expressed resentments against discrimination and everyday injustice. This motivated them to participate in strife, riots and movements. Thus fraternal deprivation at group level was found. Caplan and Paige (1968) conducted study on whit-black relationship on the basis of Detroit and New York riot. They reported that prolonged exclusion of Negroes from American economic, political and social life was the cause for violent reaction of Negroes towards white. Whites were powerful outgroup and they were blamed for being racial discrimination as a barrier to Negro progress. Hence, Negroes blamed the White for racial discrimination and reacted violently to improve their conditions.

Gurin, Gurin, Lao and Beatlic (1969) found a marked tendency for militancy among Negro students to be associated with the belief that they could not reach personal goal because of systematic social constraints. In other study, Meyer (1968) conducted a study on Miami-areas Negroes.

The purpose of this study was to explore the relationship between militancy and political efficacy in intergroup behavior. It was found that Miami-area Negroes who scored high on militancy were found to exhibit strong feeling against discrimination. Thus the study showed positive relationship between the participant's score of militancy and their sense of personal and political efficacy. Caplan (1970) conducted a research on urban disorders. It was found that Negroes participated in riots simply because they were interested for the improvement of their position in American society. The militants were rebelling against the inequalities and contradictions for the system.

Gurr (1970) provided a causal model of relative deprivation and predicted that as relative deprivation increases, it leads to frustration and anger. These psychological states produce aggression. Thus he concluded that an increase in the possibility of violence in any society.

Murphy and Watson (1970) conducted study aboutanti-white sentiments of Negroes. They found that anti-white sentiments were most intense among those riot participants who perceived discrimination practices causing restricted economic and social mobility for Negroes. Thus they identified the cause of riot to be rooted in anger over the conditions produced and sustained by denying Negroes the same freedom and opportunities available to whites. Pettigrew (1971) found that relative deprivation was positively correlated with Cleveland riots. The Cleveland riot report also showed that increased residential segregation of blacks from whites increased the feelings of relative deprivation and thereby predisposes blacks more towards militancy.

Sears and McConahay (1970) found that relative deprivation with regards to jobs was greater in riot participants than non-participants. It indicated that the phenomena of relative deprivation were highly correlated with dissatisfaction caused by injustice due to unequal distribution of rewards and privileges in terms of monetary gain. Geschwender and Geschwender (1973) found that fraternal relative deprivation of Black as a group did predict participation in riot and group action. However, they found that the sense of past progress or future decline had no effect on riot participation. On the basis of these investigations, the investigators concluded that neither present nor future relative deprivation regard with neither best life, nor sense of past progress or future decline in such deprivation were related to participation in the civil rights movement.

McPhail (1971) conducted a study on relative deprivation. The purpose of this study was to measure the association between relative deprivation and racism. The findings of this study reported significant relationship between fraternal relative deprivation and racism.

Berkowitz (1972) conducted a survey for analyzing black urban rioting in United States. It was found that frustration and requisite situational cases were main factors for the eruption of violence. Abeles (1976) reviewed various studies in the area of relative deprivation. The objective of this review was to establish relationship between relative deprivation and violent behavior of masses. On the basis of empirical findings of different studies Abeles concluded that fraternal relative deprivation is better predictor of militancy.

Cook, Crosby and Hennigan (1977) reviewed a large number of empirical studies on relative deprivation. The purpose of this review is to collect support in favor of construct validity of egoistic relative deprivation. They found that egoistic relative deprivation was originated and directed for self improvement. Newton *et al.*, (1980) conducted a study on relative deprivation. In this study, they used retrospective as well as prospective measure of protest activity. They obtained positive relationship between retrospective/ prospective measures of protest activity, but they found no relationship with predisposition to militancy.

Isaac *et al.*, (1980) also conducted an empirical investigation on relative deprivation with black and white subjects. They observed that political protest orientation was associated with economic relative deprivation for Blacks but not for Whites. Smith (1981) conducted a study using Black subjects in Britain. The purpose of this study was to explore ethnic differences and fraternal relative deprivation. The results of this study showed that economic deprivation was greater among the Blacks in Britain.

Tripathi and Srivastava (1981) conducted a study on Muslim minority in India. They found highly deprived Muslims expressed significantly more negative outgroup attitude than low deprived Muslims. Again highly deprived Muslims expressed more positive ingroup attitude than low deprived Muslims.

Guimond and Dube-Simard (1983) examined the egoistic-fraternal distinction among Francophone in Montreal. This study focused on Francophone attitudes towards Quebec's independence and concluded that perception of intergroup inequalities and the dissatisfaction was associated with the perception of Francophone. Thus, militant nationalism in the

French-Canadian sample was related to fraternal relative deprivation.

Taylor (1980, 1988) found fraternal relative deprivation causing competitive racism. He concluded that rising expectations and lack of improved conditions were the vital cause for giving rise to dissatisfaction. Gartrell (1982, 1983) combined relative deprivation theory with labor economics to understand how blue-color workers evaluate the fairness to pay differentials. This caused them to introduce the use of block models to represent the relational features of collective justice sentiments. Martin (1982) has also studied blue-color workers' evaluations of pay differentials and has merged equity and relative deprivation theory.

Martin and Murray (1983) have also reported similar findings in their study on distributive injustice and unfair exchange. They demonstrated fraternal effects among dominant groups comparing with subordinate groups. Dion and his associates (1984) used relative deprivation theory to understand oppressed people's responses to discrimination and social inequality with Chinese participants in Toronto. Walker and Pettigrew (1984) made an overview and critical analysis of relative deprivation theory and concluded that fraternal relative deprivation is more useful in predicting militancy behavior, participation in social movement and oppressed individual attempts to change the social system.

Dion (1986) tested relative deprivation theory with gay males and lesbians as participants. This group was found relevant for testing the relative deprivation viewpoint for the lesbians that they are easily identifiable as visible ethnic minorities and discrimination against them is not illegal in most of North America and the United Kingdom. The findings of the study showed that the participants who perceived high levels of discrimination showed increased approval of militant acts and violence.

Birt and Dion (1987) conducted an extensive study on relative deprivation with 74 members of Toronto's gay male and lesbian community. The study used five measures; these were (1) Relative deprivation scale, (2) Concrete fraternal discrimination scale, (3) Militancy scale, (4) Locus of control scale, and (5) Satisfaction scale. The results indicated that CFD was the best predictor of increased militancy, decreased control and decreased satisfaction.

Gaskell and Smith (1984) proposed a model of relative deprivation. This model was subjected to empirical verification using the indices of relative deprivation. The objective of the study was to obtain a broad range of economic deprivation of employed and unemployed Black and White youth. The study used 74 Whites and 118 Black male volunteers. Data were collected through structured interviews carried out on a one-to-one basis with participants. Various indices of relative deprivation were compared and it was concluded that relative deprivation theory was applicable for Blacks but not for Whites.

The association between poverty and mental health has been widely investigated. There is, however, limited evidence of mental health implications of working poverty, despite its representing a rapidly expanding segment of impoverished populations in many developed nations. In this study, we examined whether working poverty in Switzerland, a country with substantial recent growth among the working poor, was correlated with two dependent variables of interest: psychological health and unmet mental health need.

Early psychosocial deprivation can lead to problems in social functioning, including indiscriminate behaviors, inattention/overactivity, and problems in forming adaptive social relationships with peers and adults (Chisholm, 1998; Kreppner *et al.*, 2001; Zeanah *et al.*, 2005).

Early psychosocial deprivation can lead to problems in social functioning, including indiscriminate behaviors, inattention/over activity, and problems in forming adaptive social relationships with peers and adults (Chisholm, 1998; Kreppner *et al.*, 2001; Zeanah *et al.*, 2005). These effects appear to persist long after a child is placed in a family with stable and supportive care giving. It is increasingly clear that the deficits and developmental delays that result from such deprivation have their origins in compromised brain development. In the sections below, we attempt to provide a conceptual framework for this observation.

Greenough *et al.* (1987) have argued that brain development is influenced by a combination of experience-expectant and experience-dependent mechanisms. The former refers to features of the environment that are theoretically common to all members of the species, whereas the latter refers to features of the environment that are unique to the individual. A short list of experience-expectant features of the environment might include access to a caregiver, adequate nutrition, sensory and cognitive stimulation, and linguistic input. While this list of environmental features may seem obvious, children reared in settings of profound deprivation—such as in institutions— lack most elements of what should be an "expectable" environment. This deprivation from environmental input during sensitive periods of development may lead to under specification and miswriting of circuits in the immature nervous system.

Deprivation of Liberty

Sometimes, caring for a person with dementia involves reducing their independence or restricting their free will in some way. If they are receiving care in a hospital or care home, their routine may be decided for them, and they may not be allowed to leave. If the person has not freely chosen where they will live in order to receive care, or the type of care that they receive, it is possible that this care will take away some of their freedom. In some cases, this may amount to a 'deprivation of liberty'. This is not always a bad thing, and it is often necessary when caring for someone, but it should only happen if it is in the person's best interests.

The Mental Capacity Act 2005 includes the Deprivation of Liberty Safeguards (DOLS) – a set of checks that aims to make sure that any care that restricts a person's liberty is both appropriate and in their best interests. This page explains what counts as a deprivation of liberty, what the safeguards are, and how to go about getting a deprivation of liberty authorized and reviewed. DOLS only apply for people in care homes and hospitals. There is a separate system for people in 'supported living arrangements'– where people live and receive care in the community. They also only apply to people living in England and Wales. At the time of writing (March 2016) there is no similar system in Northern Ireland (https://www.alzheimers.org.uk/get-support/legal-financial/deprivation-liberty-safeguards-dols).

The Mental Capacity Act (2005) (MCA) and Deprivation of Liberty Safeguards During the Corona Virus (COVID-19) Pandemic. This guidance is only valid during the COVID-19 pandemic and applies to those caring for adults who lack the relevant mental capacity to consent to their care and treatment. The guidance applies until withdrawn by the Department of Health and Social Care. During the pandemic, the principles of the MCA and the safeguards provided by DOLS still apply.

Decision-makers in hospitals and care homes, and those acting for supervisory bodies will need to take a proportionate approach to all applications, including those made before and during the pandemic. Any decisions must be taken specifically for each person and not for groups of people.

Where life-saving treatment is being provided, including for the treatment of COVID-19, then the person will not be deprived of liberty as long as the treatment is the same as would normally be given to any person without a mental disorder. The DoLS will therefore not apply.

It may be necessary, for a number of reasons, to change the usual care and treatment arrangements of somebody who lacks the relevant mental capacity to consent to such changes.

In most cases, changes to a person's care or treatment in these scenarios will not constitute a new deprivation of liberty, and a DOLS authorization will not be required. Care and treatment should continue to be provided in the person's best interests.

- If new arrangements constitute a 'deprivation of liberty' (many will not)
- If the new measures do amount to a deprivation of liberty, whether a new DOLS authorization may be required (in many cases it will not be)

(https://www.gov.uk/government/publications/coronavirus-covid-19-looking-after-people - who - lack - mental-capacity/the-mental-capacity-act-2005-mca-and-deprivation - of - liberty - safeguards - dols - during - the - coronavirus-covid-19-pandemic)

A review of literature relating to fraternal relative deprivation shows that social violence and protest behavior (Caplan & Paige, 1968, Gurr, 1970, Runciman, 1966) stem from perceived feelings of injustice and unequal distribution of resources. Membership in a group may contribute to the development of positive or negative social identity of an individual. People generally compare their own membership group to some other reference group. This comparison is made on some evaluative dimensions, which have clear value differentials (Commins & Lockwood, 1979). This comparison may result in legitimate or illegitimate perception of the group. Legitimate means favorable and illegitimate means unfavorable comparisons, which may be stable or unstable. When the individuals make unfavorable comparisons and it is judged to be both illegitimate and stable, it is said to be in a state of relative deprivation. The concept of relative deprivation is a kind of social evaluation theory (Pettigrew, 1967). It formalizes the relationships between social comparison groups. It leads to a variety of behavioral outcomes. When the individual's evaluation proves to be negative, the individual experiences relative deprivation. Then he is motivated to change the membership or to change the dimensions of comparison or he is directed towards revolution for changing the existing social system. Stouffer and his colleagues (1949), followed by Davis (1959) and Runciman (1966) introduced the initial concept of relative deprivation. Runciman distinguishes between Egoistic Relative Deprivation and Fraternal Relative Deprivation.

When the individual compares him with other of his own group and feels deprived in relation to them; it is called egoistic relative deprivation. Fraternal relative deprivation involves the comparison of the in-group versus outgroup and the conclusion is that the in-group is deprived. The present study is concerned with an empirical investigation of relative deprivation as related to caste, sex and residential background of Hindus of Bangladesh.

CHAPTER 2

Socio-Cultural Background of Bangladesh and West Bengal

The geographical location of West Bengal has an important bearing on its ancient history. It lies on the eastern end of the great Indo-Gangetic plain. It afforded a free and open passage to the communities who, in the ancient swarms of migration, had sought to move about and traverse its length and breadth. Some groups of these earlier immigrants had chosen to settle in Bengal permanently. Because of this, there must have been several cases of inter-racial and even inter-caste mingling and absorptions among them. Subsequently, apart from the Vedic races who dominated, Bengal presented a picture of its varied races of people composed of the Munda and Kolarian segment linguistically and racially with an Austro-Asiatic identity of their own confined westwardly; there were the Bodo races of the east and the Tibet-Burman race who occupied the mountain terrain of the Himalayas. In the course of thousands of years, Bengali had constituted itself not only the great eastern gateway but, had witnessed the convergence of the civic, cultural and social trends of a great transformation. They had contributed greatly to the social cosmopolitan character of the people in the state.

The Hindu evidently, on account of their vast and wide-spread population, predominated; they were diffused from the upper Gangetic valley. They were the descendants of their great forefathers who had played role to nurture and shape the great Vedic culture and civilization. They were the ancient follower of Hinduism propounded and propagated by the great teachers of religion; they observed the similar practices, sacrifices and festivals, their cultural and economic activities followed the same pattern which their forefathers were went to practise than in their previous home. But the local variations were inevitable due to the fact that they had to become habituated to the environs and surroundings in the great fertile plane.

Indian state of West Bengal has a population of 67,982,732 persons (1991 census). It has the fourth largest population in the country, ranking after Uttar Pradesh, Bihar and Maharashtra. The literacy rate in West Bengal as stated in Census is 57.72 percent. The growth of population after independence clearly shows a steady increase in population in West Bengal between 1951-1991. The picture was however not similar in the pre-independence days. In the past forty years of the present century population increased very slowly. It was mainly because there was not much difference in the natural birth rate and death rate. Moreover, the immigration was also at an alarming level. After partition many of the people migrated from West Bengal to East Pakistan (present Bangladesh) and vice-versa. It was after 1971, i.e. after the creation Bangladesh that the process of immigration increased substantially and the population of West Bengal increased at an unparalleled rate.

On the criterion of census of population is based on religious composition there had been substantial changes in the religious composition of the state in the last few decades as population not migrated from India to Pakistan and from

Pakistan to India. The independence of Bangladesh in 1971 also affected the religious composition of population. The religious composition data for the year of 1991 has been published by the government of India so far. It is interesting to examine religious composition of the population in the past (1931-1941). The religious composition of Bengal is given below according to the census of 1931: A. Hindus 12,246,402 against 19,510,660 in 1941, B. Muslims 4,755,520 against 5,544,380 in 1941, C. Christians 112,080 against 114008 in 1941, D. Sikhs 6,883 against 15,084 in 1941, E. Jains 6,442 against 6,170 in 1941, F. others 534,222 against 739,313 in 1941.

After partition of sub-continent the total population of Hindus in 1951 was 19,510,660 persons (63%) followed by Muslims 4,929,163 and Christians 175,293. The population of Sikhs and Jains was 29,867 and 19,116 respectively while 198,118 were under the category of others. In 1981 also the Hindus dominated the population while the Muslims stood second in numerical strength. The third position was occupied by Christians, followed by Sikhs, Jains and others. The population of all the religions is increasing almost in the same proportion but there is a belief that owing to the immigration of Muslims from Bangladesh the population of Muslims kept increasing at a relatively faster rate.

West Bengal and Bangladesh

After the partition of Bengal into East and West, the former joining with Pakistan and the latter joining with India, a good number of Hindus have migrated to West Bengal. As a result, the Hindus in east Bengal became numerically few and they occupy the lower rung of socio-economic ladder in respect of education, income, occupation, and political environments. Similarly, a large number of Bengali Muslims also have migrated from the Indian territory of West Bengal to take shelter and cultural support within the people of East Bengal (Bangladesh). At the same time, Bengali who left the West Bengal suffered scapegoat and the consequences of minority status. Further, cultural differences have made it difficult for the Hindu minority in Bangladesh and Muslim minority in West Bengal to succeed as equals in their respective society. Because of this religious discrimination members of minority groups of both countries of Bangladesh and India (West Bengal) become more noticeable in terms of language use and religious practices. As a result of this discrimination and accompanying deprivation many members of the minority groups in both the nations maintain their cultural, religious, and language distinctiveness with their respective reference groups outside the political boundary.

Both Bangladesh and India Bengali Muslims are proud of the fact that they inherit a standard culture which is further enriched by assimilating Bengali taste and temperament and in this regard Bengali language has served as an essential aspect of cultural identification in the past. But the pattern of loyalty of West Bengal Hindus is somewhat different. They are fundamentally haunted by Indian nationalism. The identification of West Bengalis with Indian nationalism has thus become associated with emotive expression towards Hinduism, which is ideally sound but conflicts on certain subjective and objective levels. Indian Bengalis concentrated themselves on merit for attaining artistic and scientific superiority and they have made considerable achievements by creating rich literature. In the scientific field their contribution is also noticeable. This new dimension of comparison has worked as a strategy of what Tajfel (1974) called 'Cognitive alternative' on the Psychological functioning of Indian Bengalis for fetching self-esteem and prestige within the fold of Indian nationalism. The simple logic for this reverse condition is that Indian Bengalis have accepted their geographical and political reality and searched for cognitive alternative in the new dimension of artistic, literary, and scientific supremacy. Indian nationalism has provided them a safeguard for a luxuriant growth and social competition.

Bengalis in Bangladesh, on the other hand, considered the geographical and political reality as colonial device for exploitation by Pakistan and concerted efforts for changing the environment through direct competition and eventually they were successful in finding a new national identity. The Muslims of Bangladesh have however, shifted their genius for creating a new dimension of comparison on linguistic differentiation for maintaining group distinctiveness.

Language policy of Bangladesh government is indicative of assimilationist forces that exist in the society and thus to make a reconciliation between Bengali and Muslim culture through linguistic modification. This effort is based on the implicit assumption that standard of language developed by Muslims is exhaustive, all inclusive, dynamic and hence superior. However, the Bengali Hindus are trying to retain their language as a mark of social identity and as such have been suffering the consequences of resisting assimilation through political, economic and cultural means. Thus it appears, that the division of Bengal in East and West was not merely a geographical and political separation, it was a semi-linguistic as well as cultural uniformity.

The Bengalis in Bangladesh, the ethnic kin group is the Bengalis in West Bengal in India. In the immediate aftermath of the partition of British India into India and Pakistan and the Bengalis in East Pakistan and the Bengalis in West Bengal was far from cordial. During the British rule of India, Bengal (then called the United Province of Bengal) was a mixed Hindu-Muslim state, with the Muslims holding a slight majority. When India became independent in 1947, the eastern part of the province (which had a Muslim majority) joined Pakistan whereas the western part became part of India in the form of the state of West Bengal. Partition of the province led to the migration of Hindus from East Pakistan to West Bengal, which thus became a predominantly Hindu province.

Hindu population of West Bengal had little sympathy for Bengali Muslims of East Pakistan for a number of reasons. First, on the eve of the partition of British India, Calcutta, the capital of the United Province of Bengal, witnessed one of the worst communal riots between Hindus and Muslims. The communal hatred caused by the riots was further intensified by the partition of the province in 1947 and the subsequent migration of over 4 million Hindu refugees from East Pakistan to West Bengal. Bengalis in West Bengal did not see the people of Pakistan as Pakistanis but as fellow Bengalis.

Partition of Bengal adversely affected the jute industry in West Bengal which was dependent on the supply of raw materials from the areas which now became East Pakistan. In 1947, 92% of the jute grown in Bengal was grown in the regions which become East Pakistan, whereas most of the jute mills were located in West Bengal.

The Bengalis in East Pakistan clashed with the Pakistan government from literally the first day over linguistic, economic and political rights. So, they stressed their ethnic identity over their religious one, i.e. they were Bengali Muslims and not Muslim Bengalis. This championship of Bengali identity was a direct challenge to the religio-ideological basis of Pakistan and it received a lot of support from Bengalis of India. The relation between the Bengalis of East Pakistan and the Bengalis of West Bengal improved significantly. Because of the agitation by the Bengalis, the Pakistani government allowed greater economic and cultural exchanges between East Pakistan and West Bengal and also relaxed restrictions on travel. Increased contacts between the sides thus dissolved some of the earlier animosities. Relations had improved as result of demographic changes in both East Pakistan and West Bengal. The coming of age of a post-independence and post-partition generation meant that the earlier hostile sentiments on both sides were gradually come back to normal. Bengalis in West Bengal were appalled by the atrocities committed by the Pakistani army in East Pakistan. The genocide that was taking place in East Pakistan after the 1970 elections created widespread hatred and anger in West Bengal towards the Pakistani government and the military. So, the people of West Bengal were sympathized towards the Bengalis in East Pakistan. The government of West Bengal created pressure on New Delhi to do something to protect the lives and properties of the Bengalis in East Pakistan. Hence, New Delhi was not in a position to ignore the sympathies of the Bengalis in West Bengal towards their ethnic kin in East Pakistan.

Partition of India

Britain's holdings on the Indian subcontinent were granted independence in 1947 and 1948, becoming four new independent states: India, Burma (now Myanmar), Ceylon (now Sri Lanka), and Pakistan (including East Pakistan, modern-day Bangladesh). Sikkim, then an independent country, is not shown on this map.

The Partition of India was a partition that led to the creation on 14 August 1947 and 15 August 1947, respectively, of the sovereign states of Dominion of Pakistan (later Islamic Republic of Pakistan) and Union of India (later Republic of India) upon the granting of independence to British India from the United Kingdom of Great Britain and Northern Ireland. In particular, it refers to the partition of the Bengal province of British India into the Pakistani state of East Bengal (later East Pakistan, now Bangladesh) and the Indian state of West Bengal, as well as the similar partition of the Punjab region of British India into the Punjab province of West Pakistan and the Indian state of Punjab.

The secession of Bangladesh from Pakistan in the 1971 Bangladesh Liberation War is not covered by the term Partition of India, nor are the earlier separations of Ceylon (now Sri Lanka) and Burma (now Myanmar) from the administration of British India. Ceylon, part of the Madras Presidency of British India from 1795 until 1798, became a separate Crown Colony in 1798. Burma, gradually annexed by the British during 1826 – 86 and governed as a part of the British Indian administration until 1937, was directly administered thereafter. Burma was granted independence on January 4, 1948 and Ceylon on February 4, 1948.

The remaining countries of present-day South Asia- Nepal and Bhutan- having signed treaties with the British designating them as independent states were never a part of British India and therefore their borders were not affected by the partition.

Partition and Emergence of Bangladesh

Bangladesh become independent from Pakistan in 1971, it marked the culmination of a very long period of nationalist struggle on the part of the Bengali people. Nationalist feelings were not new to Bengalis– ever since the formation of Pakistan; they had demanded greater regional autonomy for the East Wing. But the crystallization of Bengali nationalism into a secessionist movement geared towards the creation of a separate and independent Bengali state occurred only in early 1971. Ethno-secessionist movements of Bangladesh is however unique, because it was one of the very few cases of successful cessation by an ethnic group in the period 1947-1971. In the secessionist attempt by the Bengalis in East Pakistan, the most crucial role was played by India, the ethnic kin state of West Bengal. India accepted an enormous refugee burden from East Pakistan, also provided diplomatic, financial and military support to the Bengalis.

Bengalis nationalism in Pakistan travelled two main routes. Between 1947 and 1971, the linguistic, cultural, economic, administrative and political demands of the Bengalis were centred on achieving the greatest possible degree of regional autonomy for the East Wing. The process reached its peak with the demand by the Bengalis that except for matters of defense, communication, and foreign affairs, all other powers should belong to the provinces. In spite of repeated rebuffs by the Pakistani Govt. the Bengalis stuck to their demands for regional autonomy. It changed to demands for independence only after the Pakistani military crackdown in the East Wing in the early 1971.

Scholarly works have put forward a combination of socio-cultural, ethnic, economic, administrative and political reasons to account for the Bengalis demand for regional autonomy as well as independence. Thus, the socio-cultural and ethnic distinctiveness of Bengali people, their linguistic, economic, administrative and political exploitation at the hands of the Pakistan Govt. dominated by ethnic groups from the West Wing and geographical absurdity of Pakistan have all been stressed in order to explain the rise of Bengali nationalism.

First clash over language between the Bengalis and the central government broke out immediately after partition, the Pakistani government made Urdu the national language of Pakistan. Urdu the national language of a small minority of the people; but it was considered as the principal language of Indian Muslims and closely associated with Muslims politics in the subcontinent. The language politics of Pakistani government provided the spark to Bengali nationalism. Bengali was the language of the majority of the people of Pakistan but it was confined to the East Wing only. Moreover, the Bengali language was very different from the language in the West Wing; in fact, it is identical to the language used by the Indian province in West Bengal.

It is within this background that with the active co-operation with the Indian army (Mucktibahini) the birth of Bangladesh took place in December 1971 as a sovereign state after a nine month heroic struggle and war of liberation. It thus appears that though West Bengal and Bangladesh are distinctive political realities they share many features of a common cultural background. The salience of linguistic affinity as reflected in Bengali nationalism leading to the emergence of Bangladesh seems to override the ethnic differences, which surface intermittently due to the Hindu-

Muslim religious divide. Conflicts regarding Bangladeshi identity which lies between Islamic and Bengali nationalism would probably continue into the future. However, the cultural similarities between West Bengal and Bangladesh rooted in history provide shared standard and norms of everyday living which are more than the discontinuities emerging from more recent crystallization of the Muslim identity.

CHAPTER 3

Emergence and Development of Hindu Caste System

Traditional theory about the origin of caste has been written in the laws of Manu (Buhler, 1886). According to this Hindu tradition, the caste system owes its origin to the four *Varnas*. They are *Brahmins, Kastriya, Vaishyas* and *Sudras*. The tradition says that *Brahmin* sprang from the mouth of deity, the *Kastriya* was created from his arms, the *Vaishya* was formed from his thighs and *Sudra* was born from his feet (Wilson, 1877).

Brahmins were assigned divinity and duties of studying, teaching, sacrificing, giving alms and receiving gifts to the end that the Vedas might be protected. *Kastriya* were assigned strength and the duties of studying, sacrificing, giving alms, using weapons, protecting treasure and life to the end that good government should be assured. *Vaishya* were allotted the power of work and the duties of studying, sacrificing, giving alms, cultivating, trading and tending cattle, to the end that labour should be productive. *Sudra* was given the duty of serving the other three higher *Varnas*.

Nesfield (1885) has advocated for the occupational theory of caste system. He regards occupation as the exclusive basis of caste distinction. Blunt (1912) observe that the origin of caste must be sought for in the peculiar circumstances of a complex system of society with a cross division of guilds. Chanda (1916) also traces caste to race and function. Color or race difference, real and fancied, together with hereditary function gave birth to the caste system. Risley (1915) has relied mainly to theories of race and hypergamy to explain the caste system. He regards caste system primarily as due to color differences. According to him the intermarriage between fair invaders and dark aborigines provides enough women for the society in question to close its ranks and become a caste. Dutt (1954) has adopted Risley's theory of origin of caste and attached much more value in the code of Manu to account for the caste system.

A theory of the origin of caste, which combines both functional and racial origins, has been put forward by Slater (1981). He has suggested that caste system existed across India before the Aryan invasion as a result of occupations becoming hereditary and marriage being arranged by parents within the society of the common craft because sexual maturity an early age and trade secrets were thus preserved. As a result of magic and religious ceremonies also, exclusive occupational groups were built up and marriage outside the group became prejudicial and contrary to practice. The Aryan invasion had the effect of strengthening a tendency to associate difference of color and of strengthening also a tendency for caste to be placed on a scale of social precedence.

In spite of these interpretations an explanation about the emergence and development of caste system, it is important to note that the general Hindu feeling about the caste system is that it has been established by divine ordinance or at least with divine approval. This takes precedence of all other obligations including friendship and kindred feeling.

Thus, it is clear that the caste system is a unique social phenomenon and the factors contributing to it are varied in number. In a word, geographical and migration considerations together with matrilineal and patrilineal societies are responsible for the emergence and development of caste system. Further, the belief of mana, taboo and magic which surrounds the primitive philosophy of soul or life-matter and which have enriched the Hindus may be accounted for the creation of caste system in the Indian sub-continent.

Finally, caste system in Hinduism is a kind of social categorization and it imposes boundaries on intergroup behavior. As a result, unfavorable comparison between groups may lead to the emergence of fraternal relative deprivation. The purpose of the present study was to investigate fraternal relative deprivation as it is related to caste, sex and residential background of Bangladeshi Hindus. Thus, it is necessary to give a short theoretical description of the concept of relative deprivation.

CHAPTER 4

Development and Objective of the Study

Rationale of the Study

It is popularly believed that Sudras are not given equal status in society with the Brahmins. These discriminatory behaviors have been questioned by the modern social reformers. These discriminations in society are likely to originate the feelings of fraternal relative deprivation in Sudras. Again Brahmin and high caste Hindus in undivided Bengal had dominated Muslims in social, economic and political spheres. At present Brahmins and high caste Hindus have been deprived of their domination status. This reversal in position is likely to give birth the feelings of deprivation in Brahmins also. Thus, there are obviously some social, political and economic changes in the social structure of Bangladesh. Hence it is necessary to verify empirically these intergroup relations. The present study's findings would provide empirical knowledge and insight to the political thinkers, economic planners, and social reformers.

Hypothesis

On the basis of above discussions about the concept of relative deprivation, emergence and development of caste system and theoretical construct of relative deprivation, the present study would conduct an empirical investigation on fraternal relative deprivation as related to caste, sex and residential background of Hindus in the social, economic and political context of Bangladesh. For thi purpose, following hypotheses were formulated and their justifications were given herein:

Hypothesis 1:

Brahmin participants with high caste identity would feel gratification and *Sudra* participants with low caste identity would feel deprivation in their competitions for social, economic and political privileges.

Justification 1:

This hypothesis has been formulated in the light of social identity theory as advocated by Tajfel (1978). According to Tajfel, an individual's identity is socially determined by his/her belongingness to a group. If the group fails to provide positive social identity, then the group members feels insecure and they feel that their membership is illegitimate and unstable. This atmosphere leads to the development of the feelings of fraternal relative deprivation. Sudra participants with low cast identity in comparison to Brahmin participants with high caste identity would feel that their group as a whole is being deprived from social, economic and political privileges.

Hypothesis 2:

(*a*) In case of *Brahmin,* males would express higher feelings of gratification in comparison to females. (*b*) In case of *Sudra,* females would express higher feelings of fraternal relative deprivation in comparison to males.

Justification 2:

These hypotheses have been formulated in the perspective of socio-cultural conditions of Bangladesh. Bangladesh is a male-dominating society. It is a cultural vale in Bangladesh that females would show unconditional subjugation to males and it is perpetually observed through the marriage ceremony. In fact, Bangladesh is a traditional society and religious imposes certain sanctions that have made women subordinate to men. Thus there is obvious discrimination between rights, privileges, and social status between males and females in Bangladesh. These are more prominent in case of Hindus. The traditional Hindu society seldom grants any rights to women in the society except that she is the wife and mother and her salvation lies in the satisfaction of her husband. Because of these unique characteristics of social system, females are regarded as subordinate group in comparison to males. These observations have led to the formulation of the above two hypotheses.

Hypothesis 3:

Residential background in terms of Urban Rural origin would have differential impact on gratification as well as deprivation of the participants.

Justification 3:

Bangladesh is composed 68,000 villages, 468 upazillas and 64 districts. It indicates that majority of her population belongs to rural areas. A small portion of her population belongs to rural areas. It is observed that a good portion of urban population have come from rural population. Because of these uneven distributions of population between urban and rural areas, it is quite difficult to separate urban characteristics. In spite of that it is important to note that many social, economic and political privileges are unique in the rural context which are absent in urban context. Similarly, there are many social, economic and political privileges that are exclusively enjoyed by urban population. Hence, in spite of little differences between urban and rural population, it is expected that differentials in gratification or deprivation would be observed due to differences in situational conditions between urban and rural areas. In the perspective of these arguments, it has been hypothesized that residential background in terms of urban and rural origin would have differential impact on gratification as well as deprivation of the participants.

It is clear that caste system in Hinduism is a kind of social categorization and it imposes boundaries on intergroup behavior. As a result, unfavorable comparison between groups may lead to the emergence of fraternal relative deprivation. The purpose of the study was to investigate Fraternal Relative Deprivation as it is related to caste system, sex and residential background of Bangladeshi Hindus. Particularly high caste Brahmins and low caste Sudras were taken into consideration along with their male-female categorization and urban rural dimension.

In Bangladesh majority of her population belongs to rural areas. A small portion of her population lives in urban areas. It is observed that a good portion of urban population has come from rural population. Because of this uneven distribution of population between urban and rural areas, it is quite difficult to separate urban characteristics from rural characteristics. In spite of that it is important to note that many social, economic and political privileges are unique in the rural context, which are absent in urban context. Similarly, there are many social, economic and political privileges that are exclusively enjoyed by urban population. Hence, in spite of little differences between urban and rural population, it is expected that differentials in gratification or deprivations would be observed due to differences in situational conditions between urban and rural areas. In the perspective of these arguments, it has been hypothesized that residential background in terms of urban rural origin would have differential impact on gratification as well as deprivation of the participants.

The present study was designed to conduct an investigation on fraternal relative deprivation as related to caste, sex and residential background in the social, economic and political context of Bangladesh. The theories or relative deprivation and the review of literature have shown that fraternal relative deprivation stems from perceived inequalities in the distribution of resources and privileges on group levels. When the members of a group compare their own group with the relevant outgroup and find their own group deprived of some valuable objects or opportunities, a feeling of fraternal relative deprivation occurs. It is thus important to note that deprivation involves four steps. First, perception of inequality, second, comparison between own group and the relevant outgroup, thirdly, a belief that a discriminatory behavior is present and Fourthly, the occurrence of felt relative deprivation leading to certain behavioral actions like protest behavior, collective demonstration, group actions, etc. All these criteria of relative deprivation theory have been utilized in the present study.

The broad objective of the study was to explore the phenomenon of fraternal relative deprivation as related to caste, sex and residential background of Hindus in Bangladesh. Specific objectives of the study were as follows:

1. To show differential pattern of fraternal relative deprivation in Brahmins and Sudras due to social, political, and economic discrimination.
2. To show the patterns of deprivation in Brahmins and Sudras due to male-female categorization.
3. To compare between various forms of relative deprivation in Brahmins and Sudras as a result of urban-rural residential background.
4. To study fraternal relative deprivation in Brahmins and Sudras in relation to social, economic and political conditions of Bangladesh.

Generally speaking, Bangladesh is a monolingual country. As the name indicates Bangladesh is the homeland of Bengalis. In spite of that Bengal was divided into East and West in 1947 on the basis of religious categorization. Thus in spite of common racial origin, Bengalis was identified as Muslims and Hindus at the time of independence of India in 1947. East Bengal was renamed as East Pakistan by Pakistani rulers. However, East Pakistan emerged as an independent and sovereign state in 1971 and it has been named Bangladesh. Because of these historical events and changes, Hindus in Bangladesh constituted a minority position in social, political and economic activities. The status of Hindus further deteriorated due to their migration to Indian state of West Bengal. As a result, the Hindus in general have been subjected to the feelings of relative deprivation. The present study aims to explore the differentials in fraternal relative deprivation among various castes of Hindu community. Particularly high caste Brahmins and low caste Sudras were taken into consideration along with their male-female categorization and urban-rural division.

CHAPTER 5

Methods and Practices

Design

The present study used caste, sex and residential background as independent variables and fraternal relative deprivation as dependent variable. Accordingly, the study used a factorial design of '2 x 2 x 2' involving two levels of caste (Brahmin/Sudras), two levels of sex (Male/Female), and two levels of residential background (Urban/Rural).

Sample

The sample of the study constituted 200 participants equally divided into Brahmin and Sudras. Each group of Brahmin (n = 100) and Sudras (n = 100) was equally divided into males (n = 50) and females (n = 50). Each group of males and females was again subdivided into rural (n = 25) and urban (n = 25) origin. The participant was between 20 to 25 years of ages. The median age of the participant was 23 years. The educational level of the participants was controlled. They were collected from Rajshahi University, Rajshahi Government College and Rajshahi Medical College. The break-up of sample distribution is shown in the following table.

TABLE 1: Break-up of Sample Distribution

Residential Background	*Brahmin*		*Sudra*		*Total*
	Male	*Female*	*Male*	*Female*	
Urban	25	25	25	25	100
Rural	25	25	25	25	100
Total	50	50	50	50	200

Mode of Sample Selection

A stratified sample was used in this study. The investigator approached individually to each participant and asked about his/her caste identity. The participants who identified him/herself as Brahmin were taken as higher caste, and participants who identified him/herself as Sudra were considered low caste. All participants selected were Hindu (Brahmin & Sudra) graduate students. A participant who completed S.S.C. and H.S.C. education in villages and was born and brought up in villages was considered to have a rural background. A participant born and brought up in towns/cities and has been educated in towns, he was considered to have an urban background. Following these sample selection criteria, 25 Brahmin males of urban origin, 25 Brahmin females of urban origin, 25 males of Rural origin, and 25 Brahmin females of Rural origin were selected. Similarly, 25 Sudra males of urban origin, 25 Sudra female of Urban origin, 25 Sudra males of rural origin, and 25 Sudra females of rural origin were selected.

Materials Used

Selection of appropriate instrument was done in the context of Bangladesh. The researches on relative deprivation have been done in different countries of the world. Birt and

Dion (1987) developed several types of relative deprivation instruments. Tripathi and Srivastava (1981) and Naqvi (1974) developed fraternal relative deprivation scale covering political, economic and social areas for measuring fraternal relative deprivation of Indian Hindus and Muslims. Huq (1985) constructed fraternal relative deprivation scale for using in West Bengal and Bangladesh. Following these measures of relative deprivation, a measure of Fraternal Relative Deprivation scale was constructed for the data collection in the present study.

Fraternal Relative Deprivation (*FRD*) *Scale*: An abridged form (Huq, 1985) was used for data collection. It contained nine items covering political, economic and social areas. The items were selected on the basis of 100% agreement among the judges. The investigator collected 25 items about relative deprivation by asking open-ended questions to 10 Brahmin and Surda students of Rajshahi University. The items were relation to political, economic and social privileges enjoyed by them in Bangladesh. The split-half reliability, corrected by Spearman-Brown prophecy formula was 0.89. Selection of the appropriate instrument was done in the context of Bangladesh.

Thus, the FRD scale contains 9 items. The Participants were asked to read each item carefully and to make a response on 11 point's scale ranging from 0 to 10. The participants were required to think twice on each item. First, he has to give his attitudinal preference for his own group and secondly, he has to give his own opinion about the relevant outgroup for the same item. Items were regarding some social, political and economic privileges. Each item was framed under some hypothetical situations. Thus, the highest possible score for the scale was (10x9) = 90 and the lowest possible score was (0x9) = 0.

Procedure

The FRD scale was used for data collection. Each participant was asked to give a judgment for each statement in terms of percentage about certain privileges in political, social and economic areas by the group concerned in relation to relevant outgroup. There was no time limit, but the participants were asked to complete the task as early as possible. Each participant judged about the possibility of getting certain political and social privileges for his own group and relevant outgroup in terms of percentage.

CHAPTER 6

Analysis and Results

The present chapter reports the results of the study. It has been reported in two parts. In the first part, Analysis of Variance (ANOVA) was computed. In the second part, mean differences were computed using "t" tests. Before the presentation of result, it should be noted that some principles were adopted for the preparation of the results. As a way of collecting data, each participant was required to give his judgment about the possibility of getting certain political, social and economic privileges for his own group in comparison to relevant outgroup in terms of percentage. In this study, Brahmins were asked to compete with the Sudras on the same valued object and vice versa.

A discrepancy score ('D' score) was obtained by subtracting outgroup possibility from own group possibility. A score with minus (–) sign was considered as deprivation score and a score with plus (+) sign was considered as gratification score. A constant of 100 was added with each score to eliminate minus (–) sign. The data was analyzed using ANOVA with independent variables of caste, sex and residential background and a dependent variable of 'D' scores.

Part-1: In this part, analysis of variance was computed

TABLE 2: Summary of factorial ANOVA involving Caste, Sex and Residential background

Sources of Variation	*SS*	*df*	*MS*	F	*Level of Significance*
Caste (A)	36073.00	1	36073.00	57.97**	0.01
Sex (B)	141.10	1	141.10	0.23	n.s.
Residential Background (C)	640.80	1	640.80	1.03	n.s.
AB	2664.50	1	2664.50	4.28*	0.05
AC	3.90	1	3.90	0.01	n.s.
BC	808.10	1	808.10	1.30	n.s.
ABC	2421.63	1	2421.63	3.89*	0.05
Within Cell (Exp error)	119474.80	192	622.27		
Total	162227.83	199			

The result of the Table-2 showed that the main effect for caste was significant F (1,192) = 57.97, p <.01, MSE = 622.27; Brahmin participants with high caste identity expressed significantly more gratification M = 16.99, SD = 1.23, while Sudra participants with low caste identity revealed significantly more deprivation M = –9.87, SD = 1.03. There was no significant difference in deprivation score as a function of sex. A two-way interaction between cast and sex F (1,192) = 3.89, p <.05 were found statistically. However, main effects for sex and residential background were non significant. Interaction effects involving caste and residential background as well as sex and residential background were found non significant.

Main Effect

The main effect of caste was significant F (1,192) = 57.97, p <.01, MSE = 622.27; Brahmin participants with high caste identity expressed significantly more gratification (M = 16.99, SD = 1.23), while Sudra participants with low caste identity revealed significantly more deprivation (M = –9.87, SD = 1.03). There was no significant difference in deprivation score as a function of gender.

Interaction Effect

A two-way interaction between caste and sex was statistically significant F (1,192) = 4.28, p <.05, Brahmin: Male M = 19.50, SD = 1.98, Female M = 14.18, SD = 1.23, Sudra: Male M = –14.36, SD = 1.79, Female M = -5.38, SD = 1.49. The three-way interaction between caste, sex and residential background was significant F (1,192) = 3.89, p <.05, Brahmin: Urban Male M = 20.40, SD = 1.24, Urban Female M = 17.44, SD = 1.01, Rural Male M = 19.20, SD = 0.82, Rural Female M = 10.92, SD = 0.59 and for Sudra: Urban Male M = –7.36, SD = 1.15, Urban Female M = -9.08, SD = 1.27, Rural Male M = –21.36, SD = 0.89, and Rural Female M = -1.68, SD = 0.09.

CHAPTER 7

Discussion and Conclusion

The present study was designed to explore the phenomenon of fraternal relative deprivation and an attempt was made to make a comparative study between Brahmin and Sudra Participants of Hindu community in social, political and economic areas in Bangladesh. It was found that Hindus were subdivided into various castes of which Brahmins regarded as higher caste and Sudras regarded as lower caste. This unequal status relationship has direct relevance with the theory of intergroup relation- such as social identity theory (Tajfel, 1978), relative deprivation theory (Stouffer *et al.*, 1949), social comparison theory (Festinger, 1954) etc.

It was found that regardless of sex and residential background the Brahmin participants expressed significantly higher feeling of gratification and Sudra participants expressed significantly higher feelings of deprivation. It indicates that Brahmin as higher caste feel that they are entitled to some privileges in the society to which Sudra as low caste should not be allowed to enjoy such privileges. Sudras on the other hand feel that their obvious inequality and injustice in society done by the high caste Hindus and the privileges granted to the high caste Hindus are not fair. These feelings of injustice and inequality may be accounted for the felt fraternal relative deprivation in Sudra Hindus. In other words, Sudras as low caste Hindus feel that they have capability and fitness similar to the Brahmins as high caste Hindus and they are prevented to utilize their capability and fitness in the society. All these findings provide confirmation to the hypothesis that Brahmin participants with high caste identity would feel gratification and Sudra participants with low caste identity would feel deprivation in their competitions for social, political and economic privileges.

In case of male-female differentiation, it was found that male participants with Brahmin identity expressed significantly higher feelings of gratification as compared to their female counterparts. Similarly, male participants of Sudra identity perceived significantly higher fraternal relative deprivation than their female counterparts. Thus, the findings related to male-female comparisons of Brahmin support the hypothesis that in case of Brahmin, males would express higher feelings of gratification in comparison to females. But the second part of the hypothesis that Sudra females would express higher feelings of fraternal relative deprivation in comparison to males was not supported by the findings. However, the results supported the opposite view that Sudra males showed significantly higher feelings of fraternal relative deprivation than the female counterparts. It is perhaps; males are not concern about the social privileges like the females. Consequently, it may be argued that Sudra males compare themselves with the Brahmin males and it is not applicable for the females. It is therefore plausible to say that the relative deprivation in Sudra females is more egoistic and less fraternal in nature.

A differential pattern of gratification as well as deprivation was obtained for residential background. It was found that Brahmin male participants of urban residential background expressed significantly higher feelings of gratification as compared to rural male, urban female and rural female participants. Again, Sudra male participants of rural residential background showed significantly higher feelings of fraternal relative deprivation as compared to urban female, urban male, rural female participants. These findings provide empirical supports for the hypothesis that residential background in terms of urban and rural origin would have a differential impacts on gratification as well as deprivation of the participants.

Further, the results of the study have provided some additional information's that are relevant with the feelings of gratification and deprivation. For example, Brahmin male participants of urban origin expressed significantly more feelings of gratification as compared to female. But no such differential pattern was obtained for Sudra participants in economic areas on deprivation scores. Similarly, Brahmin male participants of rural origin expressed significantly more feelings of gratification than their counterparts in social areas. But no such difference was obtained for Sudra participants in economic areas. However, no significant mean differences were obtained for Brahmin participants on gratification scores and Sudra participants on deprivation scores in political areas. These empirical findings seem to indicate that economic and social privileges are more important and valuable dimension for comparison between Brahmin and Sudra Hindus than the political areas. In other words, economic and social benefits have direct relevance for the upliftment of social status than the political gains for Brahmin and Sudra Hindus in socio-economic and political context of Bangladesh.

These findings lend strong support to social identity theory that disadvantaged groups will engage in direct competition with dominant group if they perceive intergroup boundaries to be impermeable, if they perceive their lower status to be illegitimate and unstable, and if they can conceive of a new status quo that is achievable (Ellemers, 1993; Hogg & Abrams, 1988; Tajfel & Turner, 1979, Huq & Saha, 1992). According to research by Wright, Taylor, and Moghaddam (1990), if the members of a disadvantaged group believe that entry to an advantaged group is open, even only slightly open (only a token percentage of people can pass), they shown collective action and individually try to gain entry to the advantaged group. Collective action is most likely to be taken when entry to the advantaged group is closed, and then those who believe they were closest to entry, because they feel the strongest sense of relative deprivation only take it.

Following fraternal relative deprivation as well as perceived gratification in Sudra and Brahmins is obvious. In fact, the Sudra has polarized around the feelings of deprivation and the Brahmins have polarized around the feelings of gratification. Thus, it is evident that the division of Hindus into high caste Brahmins and low caste Sudras is group-oriented. As a result, high caste and low caste Hindu representing Brahmins and Sudras exhibit such psychological phenomena as group members. Competitive as well as discriminative behaviors were also found to work as separate group entities. Because of these predisposing causal factors, the feelings of gratification or deprivation were found to occur.

Finally, it can be said that the present study was not amply sufficient to explore the multi-facet aspect of relative deprivation. To understand the phenomenon of fraternal relative deprivation of Bangladeshi Hindus, it is necessary to utilize multi-dimensional factors and it needs extensive empirical verification.

Bibliography

Abeles, R.D. (1976). Relative deprivation, rising expections and black militancy. *Journal of Social Issues, 32,* 119-137.

Asparouhov, T., and Muthén, B. (2010). Weighted Least Squares Estimation with Missing Data. Available online at: http://www.statmodel.com/download/ Gstruc Missing Revision.pdf

Belacchi, C., and Farina, E. (2010). Prosocial/hostile roles and emotion comprehension in pre- schoolers. Aggress. *Behav. 36,* 371–389. doi: 10.1002/ab.20361

Bellanti, C.J., and Bierman, K.L. (2000). Disentangling the impact of low cognitive ability and inattention on social behavior and peer relationships. *J. Clin. Child Psychol. 29,* 66–75. doi: 10.1207/S15374424jccp2901_7

Berkowitz, L. (1972). Frustation, comparison and other sources of emotional arousal as contributors to social unrest. *Journal of Social Issues, 28,* 77-91.

Berkowitz, L. (1989). Frustration–aggression hypothesis: examination and reformulation. *Psychol. Bull. 106,* 59–73. doi: 10.1037/ 0033-2909.106.1.59

Birt, C.M., and Dion, K.L. (1987). Relative deprivation theory and responses to discrimination in a gay male and lesbian sample. *British Journal of Social Psychology, 26,* 139-145.

Blunt, E.A.H. (1911). Report on the Census of the United Provinces of Agra and Oudh, (vol. XV pt. 1, of the Census of India, 1911). Allahabad, 1912 (cited as Census of the U.P.).

Boe, T., Overland, S., Lundervold, A.J., and Hysing, M. (2012). Socioeconomic status and children's mental health: results from the bergen child study. *Soc. Psychiatry Psychiatr. Epidemiol. 47,* 1557–1566. doi: 10.1007/s00127-011-0462-9

Boss, P., Bryant, C.M., and Mancini, J.A. (2017). *Family Stress Management: A Contextual Approach,* 3rd Edn. Thousand Oaks, CA: Sage.

Bradshaw, P., Knudsen, L., and Mabelis, J. (2015). Growing Up in Scotland: The Circumstances and Experiences of 3-Year-Old Children Living in Scotland in 2007/08 and 2013. Edinburgh: The Scottish Government.

Bronfenbrenner, U. (1977). Toward an experimental ecology of human development. Am. Psychol. 32, 515–531. doi: 10.1037/0003-066X.32.7.513.

Brown, T.A. (2015). *Confirmatory Factor Analysis for Applied Research,* 2nd Edn. New York, NY: Guilford Press.

Buhler, G. (1986). *The Laws of Manu. Translated with extracts from seven commentaries* (vol. XXV), Oxford: Oxford University Press.

Byrne, B.M. (2012). *Structural Equation Modeling with Mplus: Basic Concepts, Applications, and Programming.* New York, NY: Taylor & Francis Group.

Caplan, N., and Paige J.M. (1968). A study of gehetto rioters. *Scientific America, 219,* 15-22.

Chanda, R. (1916). The Indo-Aryan Races: A study of the origin of Indo-Aryan People and Institutions, Allahabad: Allhabad University Press.

Chaplan, N. (1970). The new ghetto man: A review of recent empirical studies. *Journal of Social Issues, 26,* 59-73.

Chen, F.F. (2007). Sensitivity of goodness of fit indexes to lack of measurement invariance. *Struct. Equ. Model. 14,* 464–504. doi: 10.1080/10705510701301834

Cheung, G.W., and Rensvold, R.B. (2002). Evaluating goodness-of-fit indexes for testing measurement invariance. *Struct. Equ. Model. 9,* 233–255. doi: 10.1207/S15328007SEM0902_5

Cohen, J. (1988). *Statistical Power Analysis for the Behavioral Sciences.* 2nd Edn. New York, NY: Academic Press.

Commins, B., and Lockwood, J. (1979). The effects of status differences favored treatment and equity on intergroup comparisons. *European Journal of Social Psychology, 9,* 281-296.

Conger, R.D., Conger, K.J., and Martin, M.J. (2010). Socioeconomic status, family processes and individual development. *J. Marriage Fam. 72,* 685–704. doi: 10.1111/j.1741-3737.2010.00725.x

Cook, T.D., Crosby, F., and Hennigan, K. (1877). The construct validity of relative deprivation. In J. Suls and R. Miller (Eds.), *Social Comparison Processes,* Washington D.C.: Hemisphere.

Costello, E.J., Compton, S.N., Keeler, G., and Angold, A. (2003). Relationships between poverty and psychopathology: a natural experiment. *J. Am. Med. Assoc. 290,* 2023–2029. doi: 10.1001/jama.290.15.2023

Davidov, E., Datler, G., Schmidt, P., and Schwartz, S.H. (2011). "Testing the invariance of values in the Benelux countries with the European social survey: accounting for ordinality," in Cross-Cultural Analysis: Methods and Applications, *eds E. Davidov, P. Schmidt, and J. Billiet* (New York, NY: Routledge), 149–172.

Davis, J.A. (1959). Formal interpretation of the theory of relative deprivation. *Sociometry, 22,* 280-296.

Dearing, E., McCartney, K., and Taylor, B.A. (2006). Within-child associations between family income and externalizing and internalizing problems. *Dev. Psychol. 42,* 237–252. doi: 10.1037/0012-1649.42.2.237

Dion, K.L. (1986). Response to Perceived Discrimination and Relative Deprivation. In J.M. Olson, C.P. Herman and M.P. Zanna (Eds.) *Relative Deprivation and Social Comparison.* The Ontario Symposium.

Dion, K.L., Dion, K.K., and Pak, A.W.P. (1984). Correlates of Perceived Prejudice in Toronto's Chinese Community. Unpublished Manuscript, University of Toronto.

Dutt, N.K. (1954). *Origin and Growth of Caste in India.* Calcutta.

Ellemers, N. (1993). The influence of socio-structural variables on identity management strategies. *European Review of Social Psychology, 4,* 27-57.

Elliott, C.D., Smith, P., and McCulloch, K. (1997). *The British Ability Scales II.* Windsor, UK: NFER-NELSON Publishing Company.

Evans, G.W., and Kim, P. (2007). Childhood poverty and health: cumulative risk exposure and stress dysregulation, 953–957. doi: 10.1111/j.1467-9280.2007.02008.xPubMed Abstract CrossRef Full Text | Google Scholar, Fairchild, G., Hagan, C. C., Walsh, N. D., Passamonti.

Fanti, K.S., and Henrich, C.C. (2010). Trajectories of pure and co-occurring internalizing and externalizing problems from age 2 to age 12: findings from the National Institute of Child Health and Human Development study of early child care. *Dev. Psychol. 46,* 1159–1175. doi: 10.1037/a0020659

Farah, M.J., Shera, D.M., Savage, J.H., Betancourt, L., Giannetta, J.M., Brodsky, N.L., *et al.* (2006). Childhood poverty: specific associations with neurocognitive development. *Brain Res. 1110,* 166–174. doi: 10.1016/j.brainres.2006.06.072

Fergusson, D.M., Horwood, L.J., and Ridder, E.M. (2005). Show me the child at seven: the consequences of conduct problems in childhood for psychosocial functioning in adulthood. *J. Child Psychol. Psychiatry 46,* 837–849. doi: 10.1111/j.1469-7610.2004.00387.x

Festinger, L.A. (1954). Theory of social comparison processes. *Human Relations, 7,* 117-140.

Galler, J.R., Bryce, C.P., Waber, D.P., Hock, R.S., Harrison, R., Eaglesfield, D., *et al.* (2012). Infant malnutrition predicts conduct problems in adolescents. *Nutr. Neurosci. 15,* 186–192. doi: 10.1179/1476830512Y.0000000012

Gartell, C.D. (1982). On the visibility of wage referents. *Canadian Journal of Sociology, 7,* 117-143.

Gartrell, C.D. (1983). Relational and Distributional Models of Collective Justice Sentiments, paper presented at the second international conference on Justice and Law, Nags Head, NC, USA, 12-18 June, 1983. Department of British Columbia, Victoria, Canada.

Gaskell, G., and Smith, P. (1984). Alienated black youth: an investigation of conventional wisdom explanations. *New Community, 9,* 182-193.

Gershoff, E.T., Aber, J.L., Raver, C.C., and Lennon, M.C. (2007). Income is not enough: incorporating material hardship into models of income associations with parenting and child development. *Child Dev. 78,* 70–95. doi: 10.1111/j.1467-8624.2007.00986.x

Geschwender, B.N., and Geschwender, J.A. (1973) Relative deprivation and participation in the civil rights movements. *Social Science Quarterly, 54,* 403-411.

Goldsmith, H.H., Buss, K.A., and Lemery, K.S. (1997). Toddler and childhood temperament: expanded content, stronger genetic evidence, new evidence for the importance of environment. *Dev. Psychol. 33,* 891–905. doi: 10.1037/0012-1649.33.6.891

Goodman, R. (1997). The strengths and difficulties questionnaire: a research note. J. Child Psychol. *Psychiatry 38,* 581–586. doi: 10.1111/j.1469-7610.1997.tb01545.x

Guimond, S., and Dube-Simard, L. (1983). Relative deprivation theory and the Quebec Nationalist Movement: The cognition emotion distinction and the personal-group deprivation issue. *Journal of Personal and Social Psychology,* 44(3), 528-535.

Guo, G., and Harris, K.M. (2000). The mechanisms mediating the effects of poverty on children's intellectual development. *Demography 37,* 431–447. doi: 10.1353/dem.2000.0005

Gurin. P., Gurin G., Lao, R.C., and Boatlic, M. (1969). Internal and external control in the motivational dynamics of Negro control in the motivational dynamics of Negro youth. *Journal of Social Issues, 25,* 29-53.

Gurr, T.R. (1970). *Why men Rebel?* Princeton, NJ: Princeton University Press.

Henry, J.D., and Crawford, J.R. (2005). The short-form version of the Depression Anxiety Stress Scales (DASS-21): construct validity and normative data in a large non-clinical sample. *Br. J. Clin. Psychol. 44,* 227–239. doi: 10.1348/014466505X29657

Hill, V. (2005). Through the past darkly: a review of the british ability scales second edition. *Child Adolesc. Ment. Health 10,* 87–98. doi: 10.1111/j.1475-3588.2004.00123.x

Hogg, M.A., and Abrams, D. (1988). *Social identifications: A social psychology of intergroup relations and group processes.* London: Routledge.

Hu, L., and Bentler, P.M. (1999). Cutoff criteria for fit indexes in covariance structure analysis: conventional criteria versus new alternatives. *Struct. Equ. Model. 6,* 1–55. doi: 10.1080/10705519909540118

Huq, M., and Saha, A.K. (1992). Environmental effect on perceived fraternal relative deprivation. *Psychological Research Journal, 16,* 59-63.

Huq, M.M. (1985). A Study in Social Identity of Certain Ethnic Groups in India and Bangladesh, A D.Phil. Dissertation, Allahabad University, Uttar Pradesh, India.

Huq, M.M. (1988). Fraternal relative deprivation of Bangladeshi students as related to sex and residential background. *The Rajshahi University Studies, 19 (part- B).*

Huq, M.M. (1991). Fraternal relative deprivation of Bangladeshi students as related to sex and residential background. *The Rajshahi University Studies (part-B), 7,* 160-176.

Issac, L., Muertan, E., and Stryker, S. (1980). Political protest orientation among black and white adults. *American Sociological Review, 45,* 191-213.

Kamata, A., Nese, J.F.T., Patarapichayatham, C., and Lai, C.F. (2012). Modeling nonlinear growth with three data points: illustration with benchmarking data. *Assess. Eff. Interv. 38,* 105–116. doi: 10.1177/1534508412457872

Kenny, D.A. (2016). Mediation. Available online at: http://davidakenny.net/cm/mediate.htm #IE

Kersten, P., Czuba, K., McPherson, K., Dudley, M., Elder, H., Tauroa, R., *et al.* (2016). A systematic review of evidence for the psychometric properties of the strengths and difficulties questionnaire. *Int. J. Behav. Dev. 40,* 64–75. doi: 10.1177/0165025415570647

Kiernan, K.E., and Huerta, M.C. (2008). Economic deprivation, maternal depression, parenting and children's cognitive and emotional development in early childhood. Br. *J. Sociol. 59,* 783–806. doi: 10.1111/j.1468-4446.2008.00219.x

Kim-Cohen, J., Moffitt, T.E., Taylor, A., Pawlby, S.J., and Caspi, A. (2005). Maternal depression and child antisocial behavior: nature and nurture effects. *Arch. Gen. Psychiatry 62,* 173–181. doi: 10.1001/archpsyc.62.2.173

L., Calder, A.J., and Goodyer, I.M. (2013). Brain structure abnormalities in adolescent girls with conduct disorder. J. Child Psychol. *Psychiatry 54,* 86–95. doi: 10.1111/j.1469-7610.2012.02617.x

Linver, M.R., Brooks-Gunn, J., and Kohen, D.E. (2002). Family processes as pathways from income to young children's development. *Dev. Psychol. 38,* 719–734. doi: 10.1037/0012-1649.38.5.719

Little, T.D. (2013). *Longitudinal Structural Equation Modeling.* New York, NY: Guilford Press.

Lovibond, P.F., and Lovibond, S.H. (1995). The structure of negative emotional states: comparison of the Depression Anxiety Stress Scales (DASS) with the beck depression and anxiety inventories. *Behav. Res. Ther. 33,* 335–343. doi: 10.1016/0005-7967(94)00075-U

Lunkenheimer, E.S., Dishion, T.J., Shaw, D.S., Connell, A., Gardner, F., Wilson, M.N., *et al.* (2008). Collateral benefits of the family check up on early childhood school readiness: indirect effects of parents' positive behaviour support. *Dev. Psychol. 44,* 1737–1752. doi: 10.1037/a0013858

Lupien, S.J., King, S., Meaney, M.J., and McEwen, B.S. (2001). Can poverty get under your skin? Basal cortisol levels and cognitive function in children from low and high socioeconomic status. *Dev. Psychopathol. 13,* 653–676. doi: 10.1017/S0954579401003133

MacKinnon, D.P., Fairchild, A.J., and Fritz, M.S. (2007). Mediation analysis. *Annu. Rev. Psychol. 58,* 593–614. doi: 10.1146/annurev.psych.58.110405.085542

Marsh, H.W., Hau, K., and Wen, Z. (2004). In search of golden rules: comment on hypothesis testing approaches to setting cutoff values for fit indexes and dangers in overgeneralizing Hu and Bentler's (1999) findings. *Struct. Equ. Model. 11,* 320–341. doi: 10.1207/s15328007sem1103_2

Martin, J. (1981) Relative Deprivation: A theory of distributive injustice for and Era of Shrinking Resources. *Research in Organizational Behavior, 3,* 53-107.

Martin, J., and Murray, A. (1983). Distributive injustice and unfair exchange. In K.S. Cook and D.M. Mesick (Eds.), *Theories of Equality: Psychological Perspective,* New York: Praeger.

Masten, A.S., Roisman, G.I., Long, J.D., Burt, K.B., Obradovic, J., Riley, J.R.; (2005). Developmental cascades: linking academic achievement and externalizing and internalizing symptoms over 20 years. *Dev. Psychol. 41,* 733–746. doi: 10.1037/0012-1649.41.5.733

Mayer, S.E. (1997). *What Money Can't Buy: Family Income and Children's Life Chances.* Cambridge, MA: Harvard University Press.

Mayer, S.E. (2002). *The Influence of Parental Income on Children's Outcomes.* Wellington, NZ: Knowledge Management Group, Ministry of Social Development.

Mazza, J.R., Pingault, J.B., Booij, L., Boivin, M., Tremblay, R., Lambert, J., *et al.* (2016). Poverty and behavior problems during early childhood: the mediating role of maternal depression symptoms and parenting. *Int. J. Behav. Dev.* doi: 10.1177/0165025416657615.

McCubbin, H.I., Joy, C.B., Cauble, E.A., Comeau, J.K., Patterson, J.M., and Needle, R.H. (1980). Family stress and coping: a decade review. *J. Marriage Fam. 42,* 855–871. doi: 10.2307/351829

McPhail, C. (1971). Civil disorder participation: A critical examination of recent research. *American Sociological Review, 36,* 1058-1073.

Meredith, W.M., and Tisak, J. (1990). Latent curve analysis. *Psychometrika 55,* 107–122. doi: 10.1007/BF02294746

Mesman, J., Stoel, R., Bakermans-Kranenburg, M.H., van IJzendoorn, M.H., Juffer, F., Koot, H.M. (2009). Predicting growth curves of early childhood externalizing problems: differential susceptibility of children with difficult temperament. *J. Abnorm. Child Psychol. 37,* 625–636. doi: 10.1007/s10802-009-9298-0

Meyer, P. (1986). *Negro Militancy and Martin Luther King: The Aftermath of Martyrdom.* Washington, D.C.: Knight Newspaper.

Montroy, J.J., Bowles, R., Skibbe, L.E., and Foster, T.D. (2014). Social skills and problem behaviors as mediators of the relationship between behavioral self-regulation and academic achievement. *Early Child Res. Q. 29,* 289–309. doi: 10.1016/j.ecresq.2014.03.002

Morris, P.A., and Gennetian, L.A. (2003). Identifying the effects of income on children's development using experimental data. *J. Marriage Fam. 65,* 716–729. doi: 10.1111/j.1741-3737.2003.00716.x

Murphy, R.J., and Watson, J.W. (1970). The structure of discontent: The relationship between social structure, grievance and riot support. In N. Cohen (Eds.), *The Los Angeles Riots: A Socio-Psychological Study,* New York: Praeger.

Muthén, L.K., and Muthén, B.O. (2012). *Mplus User' Guide, 7th Edn.* Los Angeles, CA: Muthén & Muthén.

Naqvi, N. (1974). *Relative Deprivation and Attribution of Blame.* Unpublished D. Phil. Thesis, Allahabad University, Uttar Pradesh, India.

Nese, J.F.T. (2013). *Statistical Test for Latent Growth Nonlinearity with Three Time Points. National Center on Assessment and*

Accountability for Special Education (*NCAASE*). Available online at: http://ncaase.com/publications/in-briefs

Nesfield, J.C. (1885). *Brief view of the caste system of the North-West provinces and Oudh,* Allahabad University Press.

Newton, J.W., Mann, L., and Geary, D. (1980). Relative deprivation dissatisfaction and militancy: A field study in a protest crowd. *Journal of Applied Social Psychology, 10,* 384-397.

Noble, K.G., Norman, M.F., and Farah, M.J. (2005). Neurocognitive correlates of socioeconomic status in kindergarten children. *Dev. Sci. 8,* 74–87. doi: 10.1111/j.1467-7687.2005.00394.x

Olds, D. (2002). Prenatal and infancy home visiting by nurses: from randomized trials to community replication. *Prev. Sci. 3,* 153–172. doi: 10.1023/A:1019990432161

Ornaghi, V., Brazzelli, E., Grazzani, I., Agliati, A., and Lucarelli, M. (2017). Does training toddlers in emotion knowledge lead to changes in their prosocial and aggressive behavior toward peers at nursery? *Early Educ. Dev. 28,* 396–414. doi: 10.1080/10409289.2016.1238674

Pettigrew, T.C. (1967). *Social evaluation theory: convergences and applications.* Nebraska: University of Nebraska Press.

Pettigrew, T.F. (1964). *A Profile of the Negro American.* Princeton: Van Nostrand.

Preacher, K. J., and Kelley, K. (2011). Effect size measures for mediation models: quantitative strategies for communicating indirect effects. *Psychol. Methods 16,* 93–115. doi: 10.1037/a0022658

Reid, M. J., Webster-Stratton, C., and Baydar, N. (2004). Halting the development of externalizing behaviors in head start children: the effects of parenting training. *J. Clin. Child Adolesc. 3,* 3279–3291. doi: 10.1207/s15374424jccp3302_10 CrossRef Full Text

Rhee, S.H., and Waldman, I.D. (2002). Genetic and environmental influences on antisocial behavior: a meta-analysis of twin and adoption studies. *Psychol. Bull. 128,* 490–529. doi: 10.1037/0033-2909.128.3.490

Rijlaarsdam, J., Stevens, G.W.J.M., van der Ende, J., Hofman, A., Jaddoe, V.W.V., and Mackenbach, J.P. (2013). Economic disadvantage and young children's emotional and behavioral problems: mechanisms of risk. *J. Abnorm. Child Psychol. 41,* 125–137. doi: 10.1007/s10802-012-9655-2

Risley, H.H. (1891). *Tribes and Castes of Bengal: Ethnographic Glossary.* Calcutta (Cited as Tribes and Castes).

Risley, H.H. (1915). The People of India. (The edition used here is that of 1915 edited by Crooke).

Runciman, W.C. (1966). *Relative deprivation and social justice.* London: Penguin Books.

Rutter, M., Caspi, A., and Moffitt, T.E. (2003). Using sex differences in psychopathology to study causal mechanisms: unifying issues and research strategies. *J. Child Psychol. Psychiatry 44,* 1092–1115. doi: 10.1111/1469-7610.00194

Rutter, M., Pickles, A., Murray, R., and Eaves, L. (2001). Testing hypotheses on specific environmental causal effects on behavior. *Psychol. Bull. 127,* 291–324. doi: 10.1037/0033-2909.127.3.291

ScotCen Social Research (2013). *Growing Up in Scotland: Cohort* 1, Sweeps 1-6, 2005-2011. [data collection], 11th Edn. UK Data Service. SN: 5760. Available online at: http://dx.doi.org/10.5255/UKDA-SN-5760-4

Scott, S., Knapp, M., Henderson, J., and Maughan, B. (2001). Financial cost of social exclusion: follow up study of antisocial children into adulthood. *BMJ 323:191.* doi: 10.1136/bmj.323.7306.191PubMed Abstract | CrossRef Full Text | Google Scholar

Scott, S., Sylva, K., Doolan, M., Price, J., Jacobs, B., Croo, C., *et al.* (2010). Randomised controlled trial of parent groups for child antisocial behaviour targeting multiple risk factors: the SPOKES project. *J. Child Psychol. Psychiatry 51,* 48–57. doi: 10.1111/j.1469-7610.2009.02127.x

Scottish Government (2016). *Poverty and Income Inequality in Scotland*: 2014/15. Available online at: http://www.gov.scot/Resource/0050/00502180.pdf

Searles, R., and Williams, J.A. (1962). Negro College students participant in sit-ins. *Social Forces, 40,* 215-220.

Sears, D., and McConahay, J. (1970). Racial socialization, comparison levels, and the Watts Riot. *Journal of Social Issues, 26,* 121-140.

Shaw, D.S., and Shelleby, E.C. (2014). Early-onset conduct problems: intersection of conduct problems and poverty. *Annu. Rev. Clin. Psychol. 10,* 503–528. doi: 10.1146/annurev-clinpsy-032813-153650

Skafida, V., and Treanor, M.C. (2014). Do changes in objective and subjective family income predict change in children's diets over time? Unique insights using a longitudinal cohort study and fixed effects analysis. *J. Epidemiol. Commun. Health, 68,* 534–541. doi: 10.1136/jech-2013-203308

Slater, G. (1924). *The Deprivation Element in Indian Culture.* Sage Publication: New Delhi.

Smith, D.J. (1981). *Unemployment and Racial Minorities.* London: Policy Studies Institute, No. 594.

Sosu, E.M., and Schmidt, P. (2017). Tracking emotional and behavioral changes in childhood: Does the Strength and Difficulties Questionnaire measure the same constructs across time? *J. Psychoeduc. Assess. 35,* 643–656. doi: 10.1177/0734282916655503

Stouffer, S.A., Suchman, E.A., De Vinney, L.C., Star, S.A., and Williams, R.M. (1949). *The American soldiers: adjustment during army life* (vol.1) Princeton, NJ: Princeton University Press.

Street, D., and Legget, J.C. (1961). Economic Deprivation and extremism: A study of unemployed Negroes. *American Journal of Sociology, 61*(1), 53-57.

Sun, W., Li, D., Zhang, W., Bao, Z., and Wang, Y. (2015). Family material hardship and Chinese adolescents' problem behaviors: a moderated mediation analysis. *PLoS* ONE 10:e0128024. doi: 10.1371/journal.pone.0128024

Tajfel, H. (1978). *Differentiation between social groups: Studies in social psychology in intergroup relations.* London: Academic Press.

Tajfel, H., and Turner, J. (1979). An integrative theory of intergroup conflict. In W.G. Austin and S. Worchel (Eds.), *The Social Psychology of Intergroup Relations* (33-47). Monterey, CA: Brooks/Cole.

Taylor, D.M. (1980). Ethnicity and Language: A social psychological perspective. In H. Giles, W.P. Robinson and P.M. Smith, *Language: Social Psychological Perspective.* Oxford: Pergamon.

Taylor, M.C. (1982). Improved conditions, rising expectation and dissatisfaction: A test of the past/present Relative Deprivation Hypothesis. *Social Psychology Quarterly, 45*(1), 24-33.

Tripathi, R.C., and Srivastava, R. (1981). Relative deprivation and intergroup attitudes. *European Journal of Social Psychology, 11,* 313-318.

Votruba-Drzal, E. (2006). Economic disparities in middle childhood development: does income matter? *Dev. Psychol. 42,* 1154–1167. doi: 10.1037/0012-1649.42.6.1154

Walker, I., and Pettigrew, T.F. (1984). Relative Deprivation Theory: An overview and conceptual critique. *British Journal of Social Psychology, 23,* 301-310.

Widaman, K.F., Ferrer, E., and Conger, R.D. (2010). Factorial invariance within longitudinal structural equation models: measuring the same construct across time. *Child Dev. Perspect. 4,* 10–18. doi: 10.1111/j.1750-8606.2009.00110.x

Wilson, R.C. (1877). *Indian Caste.* New Delhi: McGraw-Hill Book Co.

Wright, S.C., Taylor, D.M., and Moghaddam, F.M. (1990). Responding to membership in a disadvantaged group. Journal of Personality and Social Psychology, 58, 994-1003.

Yeung, W.J., Linver, M.R., and Brooks-Gunn, J. (2002). How money matters for young children's development: parental investment and family processes. *Child Dev. 73,* 1861–1879. doi: 10.1111/1467-8624.t01-1-00511